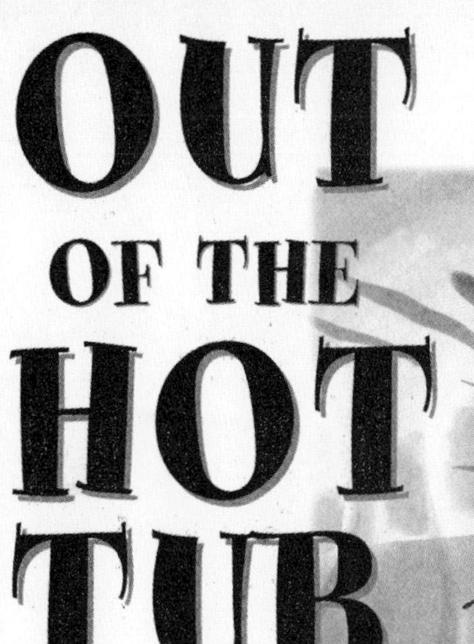

OUT OF THE HOT TUB, INTO THE WORLD

The cure for comfort-zone Christianity

KARL HAFFNER

Pacific Press® Publishing Association
Nampa, Idaho
Oshawa, Ontario, Canada
www.pacificpress.com

Edited by Tim Lale
Cover Design by Dennis Ferree
Inside Design by Steve Lanto
Cover illustration by Sandy Nichols

Additional copies of this book may be purchased at
http://www.adventistbookcenter.com

ISBN: 0-8163-1902-2

02 03 04 05 06 • 5 4 3 2 1

Contents

Dedicated

to my sermon-critique team:

DeLona Bell
Darold Bigger
John Brunt
Ernie Bursey
Nancy Canwell
Pedrito Maynard-Reid

I appreciate your faithful service to me through the years. Not only have you sharpened the following chapters, you have modeled the heart of a servant. You have shown me what the book of James looks like with skin on it. I am deeply indebted to each of you.

Special thanks to . . .

My editor, Tim Lale, for editing the muck out of my book.

My favorite encouragers—Ted and Sherry Hunter, Milt and DeDe Campbell, Max and Linnea Torkelsen, and Bob, Connie, and Dana Melashenko—for their uncanny ability to provide a breathing rainbow on cloudy days.

My relative, John L. Mack, for discovering our intersection in the family tree in—of all places—Shcherbakovka!

My fellow golf addict, Troy, for staying away from Veterans Golf Course long enough to write the study guides.

My buddies, Todd and Cherie Fletcher, who are always good for a gut-wrenching laugh.

My comfort-food cohorts, Jerry and Lisa Bryant, who have figured out how to do life.

James 1:1

Blueprint for a Better Life

"Psssssssssst! Hey, mon, wanna buy some hashish?"

The drug dealer waded through the emerald waters of Jamaica like a shark tracking unsuspecting tourists.

Clueless about his question, I floated in ignorance. It sounded to me more like a sneeze punctuated with a question mark: "Wanna buy some haaaaaaaccccchhhooooo?" This did not interest me. But my brother, Randy, knew immediately what was going down. A drug deal. An illegal transaction. An international crime.

So he reacted in a way that any normal guy who plays in the sun too long would—he busted up laughing.

"Hey, mon, what's so funny?" the dealer demanded.

"I usually don't see someone trying to peddle dope to a minister," Randy said.

"You're a minister?"

"I'm not; he is." Randy pointed at me.

"Really, you're a minister?"

My blush instantly doubled my sunburn. "Well, um, yeah, I guess I am."

"What church?"

"I'm a Seventh-day Adventist minister."

"Really? I'm a Seventh-day Adventist too!" he exclaimed.

Now I was intrigued.

"Yeah, mon! I have been a Seventh-day Adventist all my life—twenty-four years! I never miss a Sabbath in church. One time I even met our General Conference president, Elder Folkenberg."

It's not often that I'm speechless. But this was one such moment.

He grinned, "Hey, since you're a Seventh-day Adventist minister, I'll give you the same discount I give my pastor—10 percent. Come with me."

"No thanks. I don't smoke dope."

"But have you tried *this* stuff? It's a spiritual experience."

"Maybe for you, but I'm not interested."

"Come on, mon, you got to at least try it."

Back and forth we volleyed. He never could understand why I refused to buy. And I couldn't fathom how a faithful Seventh-day Adventist could make a living selling drugs.

Call me old-fashioned, but I think there ought to be some connection between what we believe and how we behave. Sadly, though, this isn't always the case. A. W. Tozer, the leathery saint of years past, once reflected on this great divide between the profession and practice of Christians. Years ago I copied this quote from a sermon by Chuck Swindoll.

> There is an evil which in its effect upon the Christian religion may be more destructive than communism, Romanism, and liberalism combined. It is the glaring disparity between theology and practice among professing Christians. So wide is this gulf that separates theory from practice in the church that an inquiring stranger who chances upon both would scarcely dream that there was any relation be-

> tween the two of them. . . . It appears to me that too many Christians want to enjoy the thrill of feeling right but are not willing to endure the inconvenience of being right.[1]

Recent statistics suggest that Christians today are faring no better. According to several recent national surveys conducted by the Barna Research Group, this chasm between theology and practice is wider than ever. Consider a slice of their findings:

- Born-again Christians spend seven times as much time on entertainment as they do on spiritual activities.
- Born-again adults are more likely to experience a divorce than are nonborn-again adults (27 percent vs. 24 percent).
- Among born-again Christian adults, only 8 percent tithe their income to the church.
- Although most believers say that serving the needy is important to do, just 34 percent gave any time and money to serve the poor in the past year.
- In a representative nationwide survey among born-again adults, none of the individuals interviewed said that the single most important goal in their life is to be a committed follower of Jesus Christ.

It seems that many of us as Christians say the right things but don't live accordingly. Whenever religion eats into the way we want to do life, it's often the spiritual stuff that gets swallowed. Too many of us camp in the world and worship our own gods.

I visited a temple in Kyoto, Japan, called The Temple of the Thousand Buddhas. It is a unique place of worship where people can literally create their own Creator. The temple is filled with more than a thousand replicas of Buddha—each one a little different from the rest. Worshipers can choose whichever god suits their fancy. It's a convenient way to mold God into the shape of their world. As the French philosopher Voltaire once wrote, "If God has created us in His image, we have more than returned the compliment." We crave a designer deity, custom-made to accommodate a faith of convenience.

Of this flavor of faith, James—the author of the epistle bearing his name—would holler, "Heresy!" Listen to his plea: "Dear brothers and sisters, what's the use of saying you have faith if you don't prove it by your actions? That kind of faith can't save anyone . . . it isn't enough just to have faith. Faith that doesn't show itself by good deeds is no faith at all—it is dead and useless" (James 2:14, 17, NLT).

It's not that works *save* the Christian, but that works *mark* the Christian. According to James, it is not enough to profess Christian values; we must live them if our faith is to be deemed authentic. To put it another way, living under the influence of God must influence the way we live.

As a driver who has been pulled over five times for driving under the influence, I know about influence. In the case of each DUI, however, I wasn't drinking. I was drowsy, or I wasn't paying attention, or I was playing the swerving game *(Let's see, how many white lines can I squeeze my tires between without touching them?)*. But to an observer, it appeared as if I was driving while under the influence of alcohol.

When people watch you, what influence do they conclude that you are under? For me, I pray for a God-intoxicated heart. I want to be constantly under His influence so that my life reflects my deepest values. My study through the book of James has deepened this resolve. I strive for the day when my thoughts might be the same as God's thoughts, my appetite His appetite, my goals His goals. I long to echo the words of Jesus and say, "If you want to know what God is like, then watch Me! Watch the way I spend My money. Watch the way I listen to people. Watch the way I react in heated situations. If you have seen Me then you have seen the Father" (see John 14:9).

While I often fall short of perfectly translating God's character through my actions, it's still the goal that James had in mind for his readers. Granted, it is an ambitious goal because translating it into life can be tricky.

As a student missionary in Swaziland, Africa, I was often asked to preach. Because I didn't speak Swahili (still don't), I preached through an interpreter. One Sabbath I shared from my heart that I believed Jesus would be coming soon. As people shuffled out of the service, though, nobody mentioned anything about the Second Coming. Instead, I received the strangest comments.

"That was an excellent sermon," someone said. "About time we hear a good old-fashioned sermon on the evils of wearing jewelry!"

Jewelry? I thought. *I never said anything about the evils of jewelry.*

Still another church member said, "Pastor, thanks for hammering on the sin of eating meat. That was a bold sermon!"

But the sermon had nothing to do with eating meat, I protested in my mind.

It wasn't until that afternoon that a close friend told me what had happened. Because my friend was fluent in both languages, he could explain the confusion. "Your interpreter was preaching his own sermon" he told me with a smile. "What he was saying had nothing to do with what you were preaching." Something was lost in the translation.

In Jesus' case, nothing was lost in the translation. His heart was intoxicated with God. He was *always* under the influence of God; consequently, His conduct mirrored his convictions. This is the challenge James gives us—to live under the Holy Spirit's influence so that we might perfectly reflect God in our lives.

That's why I beg you to sign on for this spiritual adventure through James's letter. In my opinion, it is the most practical book ever written on the topic of Christian living. The guidance is painstakingly plain for anyone who wants to serve God and lead a holy life. While many of us want that, we often stumble when it comes to pulling it off in real life.

Don't despair! James can help. He answers the fundamental question that Christians must ask: How on earth should we live? "How to manage your money"; "how to tame your tongue"; "how to overcome temptation"; and "how to pray" are just a few of the topics that James tackles. Craft your life around his counsel and you will experience an adventure with God that is out of this world. It really is a blueprint for a better life.

Before we examine the details, let's catch a quick overview of this blueprint. We'll start with the basic ABCs of the book.

It is the studied opinion of most conservative New Testament scholars that James, the brother of Christ, was the author of the epistle. In fact, in 1546, the Council of Trent acknowledged James, the brother of Jesus, as the writer. He was probably the firstborn after Jesus, making Jesus his older Brother.

Just imagine! If you have an older brother then you know how older brothers can be. Perhaps you are an older brother—shame on you! But now picture *Jesus* as your older Brother. He never sinned. He always came the first time when Mom called for supper. He always picked up His socks. He never crossed your imaginary line in the back seat of the chariot on family vacations. He always washed the ring out of the tub. He never cracked a smile when Dad did his laugh-snort thing that all dads are prone to do and everyone pretends they don't hear it.

Perfection is always a tough pill to swallow, but if your older brother is so inclined, well, that's as bad as eating Aunt Ruby's Velveeta-Wham-Tofu-Fruitcake casserole. It's no wonder that it was not until later that James became a follower of Jesus. Early on, James was hostile toward Him (see Mark 3:21, 31-35; Matthew 12:46-50; John 7:3-9). In fact, John states clearly that the brothers did not believe in Jesus (see John 7:5).

However, we see a radical change in the life of James throughout the book of Acts. He is a prominent leader in the church at Jerusalem. For example, it was to James that Peter relayed the message of his escape from prison (see Acts 12:17). James presided over the Council of Jerusalem when the Gentiles were allowed into the church. It is noteworthy that the language used in his speech at the Council is very similar to that used in the epistle of James (see Acts 15). Also, Paul came to James with his offering from the Gentile Christians to be used for the brothers and sisters in Jerusalem (see Acts 21:18-25).

Assuming the author is the brother of Jesus, then his opening statement is particularly significant: "James, a servant of God and of the Lord Jesus Christ" (James 1:1). Notice that James does not identify himself as a brother of Christ, rather as a servant. How remarkable! The brother who had once opposed Jesus was transformed into a loyal servant, shamelessly recruiting others to the cause of Christ.

The letter is written to Christians residing in Gentile communities outside Palestine. James expresses his concern for those persecuted Christians who were once part of the Jerusalem church. Many of the believers were young in their faith. Thus they needed practical instruction on how to live their personal faith in a public way. They also struggled to make sense of their persecution and pain. They were in need of counsel and encouragement, so James responded with practical help.

The book of James has been labeled the "Proverbs of the New Testament." It contains many practical, straightforward exhortations with an emphasis on the importance of balancing belief with behavior. It's about giving feet to your faith. James is very straightforward and easy to understand. In fact, at times we'll probably wish he wasn't so easy to understand!

As you read this book I anticipate significant spiritual growth. By God's grace we will not only read the words—we will do them. Listen to the final appeal that James might offer in his no-nonsense way as he invites you and me into this adventure with God.

"Pssssssssssst! Hey, mon, wanna live under the influence?"

"Huh?"

"You wanna *really* live under the influence of God and experience the supernatural?"

"Well, sure, although I am already a Christian. I believe—"

"Fair enough. Then come with me and I'll show you what your life should look like. You'll want to talk, shop, listen, pray, serve, study, dress, teach, watch TV, breathe, eat, and live in ways that are consistent with your belief."

"But—"

"No 'but's.' If you claim that you are a disciple of Christ but you do your own thing then you're deceiving yourself. If you think faith is believing one way and living another, well, then you must be smoking something funny."

James 1:2-12

Your Pain, Your Gain

I have my doubts. Some folk naturally find themselves believing stories about the far-fetched or the miraculous, but not me.

I don't believe in the Loch Ness monster. I don't believe that Elvis is mopping floors at a diner in Memphis. I don't believe that twenty-two-year-old bombshells are really in love with eighty-something billionaires. I don't believe in Princess Di conspiracy theories. I don't believe the World Wrestling Federation is a real sport. I don't believe Elizabeth Taylor will stay married next time. I don't believe the budget will ever be balanced. I don't believe that extraterrestrial beings hang out with people on this planet. That's partly because they never visit credible witnesses like a physics professor from Stanford University. Instead, aliens only seem to communicate with people who are missing their front teeth and star on *The Jerry Springer Show*. Then their parents turn out to be first cousins and I'm screaming all the louder, "I have my doubts."

Now, doubt isn't an altogether bad thing. Who wants to swallow every infomercial that comes along?

But doubt isn't an altogether good thing either. Doubts can cloud my prayer life. *God . . .where are You? Can I really trust You to take care of me?* Doubts can shrink my heart toward people. *I'd toss the man a quarter, but how do I know he won't use my money to buy booze?* Doubts can paralyze me as a person. *I'd audition for the part, but I might get rejected.*

Frederick Buechner once said, "Doubts are the ants in the pants of faith. They keep it awake and moving." That's a good quote to remember the next time you are pummeled with doubt.

Perhaps your marriage is splitting up. Maybe you have a pattern of sin in your life that feels inescapable. Maybe you've just been diagnosed with cancer and you're in a tunnel of doubt.

If so, don't get fickle in your faith. Faith is not about a doubt-free life. Nor is it a ticket on a ride devoid of pain. Sometimes faith is just hanging on in the darkness. It means depending on God through the doubt.

A couple examples of faith come to mind. Crystal's faith is firm even though her body is poisoned by cerebral palsy. She smiles easily, praises God continually, and prays daily—for those less fortunate than she.

I also think of Harold. He met God in jail while serving a double life sentence for a crime he never committed. Eventually he was pardoned and released. Just as his life was getting better, however, he was diagnosed with throat cancer. His condition now requires him to dilate his throat twice a day with an inch-thick tube that is two-and-a-half feet long. Yet despite his anguish, every day he praises God for the tube, which allows him to continue ministering to people.

He could easily allow his doubts to destroy his faith. Instead, Harold uses his doubts as fertilizer to make his faith grow.

Listen to James as he calls us to deal with doubts in the same way. "Consider it pure joy, my brothers, whenever you face trials of many kinds" (James 1:2). That is a radical statement, isn't it? How can trials be pure joy?

Recently I had a front row seat to the ultimate testing ground for trials—the delivery room. If there is a harder test anywhere, I haven't seen it. The delivery room seems the consummate metaphor for pain and trials. Now for the record, I don't criticize those people who minimize this testing phase of life. If some woman wants to deliver at home in the bathtub while all the neighbors cloister in the background singing "Kum ba Yah," that's fine by me. But for us, that was never an option.

No sooner did we arrive at the hospital than I demanded of the doctor, "Get the drugs! And if Cherié wants some, get them for her too." For the next twenty-four hours, I watched my wife survive a very testy trial. I joined the doctors and nurses around the table uttering words of encouragement and faith, even though we felt like a group of friends trying to coax a greased Saint Bernard through a cat door. It felt so impossible. Had James burst on the scene at that point and started preaching, "Consider it pure joy, my sister, for this trial that makes you feel like you're skinny-dipping in a pool of hot tar," I suspect Cherié may have uttered naughty words.

The counsel of James is what we call counterintuitive. Now really, who feels "pure joy" when facing trials? Such is not my experience. So James goes on to offer this explanation: "Because you know that the testing of your faith develops perseverance. Perseverance must finish its work so that you may be mature and complete, not lacking anything" (James 1:3, 4).

One evening Cherié and I were watching a video of Gary Smalley explaining a survey in which he interviewed hundreds of close-knit families. He asked them: "What is the best activity that your family does together that results in closeness?" Believe it or not, the most popular response was camping.

So why does camping result in bonding? According to Smalley, camping creates a non-neutral environment where it is more likely for discomforts and crises to occur. So it's not the camping that brings closeness, rather it's the experience of hardship that results in bonding.

As we were watching the video I went into the kitchen to grab something to eat. Since I was listening to the video, I spaced on the task at hand and knocked over a bottle of oil. Suddenly I was surfing in an ocean of cooking oil.

Startled, Cherié yelled from the living room, "What happened?"

"We're bonding!" I said. "I'm testing Smalley's theory. We don't have to go camping and eat tree bark and sleep with snakes—we can bond right here."

Like it or not, I think Dr. Smalley touches on a truism we're prone to deny—that trials bring benefits. They build perseverance, character, and maturity. Life is full of the kitchen-oil-spill variety of trials that can shape us into better people. John Ortberg calls them minitrials.

> Life is filled with minitrials. When someone interrupts me, I can learn to graciously hold my tongue. When my co-worker borrows something and doesn't return it immediately, I can learn patience. When I have a headache, I can discover that it is possible to suffer and not tell everybody about it. As simple as it sounds, the place to start being formed by trials is with the mini-variety.[2]

Of course we also face trials that are more like the Exxon Valdez oil spill. While these monumental challenges are intimidating, they also provide unrivaled opportunities for growth. In his book *Great Souls,* David Aikman identified the six most definitive spiritual giants of the twentieth century. The list reads like a Who's Who of hardship managers. His picks included Mother Teresa, who worked at the extreme edge of human suffering; Alexander Solzhenitsyn, chronicler of the Gulag; Elie Wiesel, Holocaust survivor; Nelson Mandela, imprisoned for twenty-seven years; Pope John Paul II, who grew up under Nazi and Communist regimes; and evangelist Billy Graham. Of the six, only Billy Graham was sheltered from extreme trials. Nevertheless, they all grew into preeminent spiritual leaders. Their stories speak volumes on the redemptive potential of hardship.

Another inspiring story is that of Stephen Hawking, the astrophysicist at Cambridge University. Many would argue that he is the most intelligent person on the planet. He has advanced the general theory of relativity beyond the bounds of anyone since Albert Einstein.

Hawking, however, is afflicted with ALS Syndrome (Lou Gehrig's disease). Eventually, the disease will claim his life. Until then, he suffers greatly under the curse. He's been confined to a wheelchair for years, where he can do little more than sit and think. And he can't speak, but must communicate by means of a computer he operates by the tiniest movement of his fingertips.

According to *Omni* magazine, "he is too weak to write, feed himself, comb his hair, fix his glasses—all this must be done for him. Yet this most dependent of all men has escaped invalid status. His personality shines through the messy details of his existence."

Before Hawking became ill, he showed minimal interest or motivation in life. He called it a "pointless existence" resulting from sheer boredom. He was a borderline alcoholic and did very little work.

Then he discovered he had Lou Gehrig's disease. The doctors informed him he would probably die within two years. The effect of that diagnosis (beyond its initial shock) was extremely positive. Hawking claims to be happier than before he got the disease.

How can that be? He explains: " 'When one's expectations are reduced to zero,' " he said, " 'one really appreciates everything that one does have.' "[3]

In other words, contentment is determined in part by what a person anticipates from life. To a man like Hawking, who knows he could die soon, everything takes on meaning—a sunrise or a walk in a park or the laughter of children.

By sailing through a hurricane-type experience, Hawking discovered a richness and texture of life that he didn't know while floating on placid waters.

Malcolm Muggeridge put it this way: "I can say with complete truthfulness that everything I have learned in my 75 years in this world, everything that has truly enhanced and enlightened my experience, has been through affliction and not through happiness."[4]

Indeed, some of the greatest human accomplishments were born out of suffering. For example, most of the Psalms were written as a result of difficulty. Most of the Epistles were written in prisons. John Bunyan wrote *Pilgrim's Progress* from jail.

Florence Nightingale, while too ill to move from her bed, reorganized the hospitals of England. And during the greater part of his life, American historian Francis Parkman suffered so acutely that he couldn't work for more than five minutes at a time. His eyesight was so poor that he could scrawl only a few gigantic words on a manuscript. Nevertheless, he authored twenty classic volumes of history.

As Tim Hansel puts it, "Sometimes it seems that when God is about to make preeminent use of a man, he puts him through the fire."[5]

So next time you spill the oil, consider it pure joy. Your pain really can be your gain. You can pass the test of trials. How? Once again let's look to James. Simply put, he instructs us to ask, then anticipate.

> If any of you lacks wisdom, he should ask God, who gives generously to all without finding fault, and it will be given to him. But when he asks, he must believe and not doubt, because he who doubts is like a wave of the sea, blown and tossed by the wind. That man should not think he will receive anything from the Lord; he is a double-minded man, unstable in all he does (James 1:5-8).

Whenever we encounter trials, our natural tendency is to ask "Why? God, why did You let this happen to me?" James suggests that we ask for wisdom instead. "God, I'm asking You to give me wisdom to see how You want me to grow through this trial."

After asking, James tells us to anticipate God's response. "But when he asks," James says, "he must believe and not doubt."

Believing without doubt, of course, does not guarantee a pain-free life. Faith is not about doubt-free certainty; it's about hanging on. Faith means walking in darkness and believing that God knows what He is doing. That's the kind of faith that builds character.

Listen to Phillip Yancey:

> For whatever reason, God has let this broken world endure in its fallen state for a very long time. For those of us who live in that broken world, God seems to value character more than our comfort, often using the very elements that cause us most discomfort as his tools in fashioning that character. A story is being written, with an ending only faintly glimpsed by us. We face the choice of trusting the Author along the way or striking out alone. Always, we have the choice.[6]

For the pilgrim who chooses to strike out alone, life becomes uncertain and tainted with doubt. James describes such a person as a wave tossed about. "He is a double-minded man, unstable in all he does." The word picture in the original language is of a staggering drunk. In other words, he can't make up his mind what to do. He is like the character in *Pilgrim's Progress* named Mr. Facing Both Ways. James would counsel you to lean into the wisdom of God. Ask God for help, then anticipate His answer in your time of trial.

James goes on:

> The brother in humble circumstances ought to take pride in his high position. But the one who is rich should take pride in his low position, because he will pass away like a wild flower. For the sun rises with scorching heat and withers the plant; its blossom falls and its beauty is destroyed. In the same way, the rich man will fade away even while he goes about his business (James 1:9-11).

Don't miss this perspective when you're tackled by trials. Guard against the upside-down value system of our culture. The world clamors for money and power and position, but why? James gently reminds us not to get sucked into a superficial way of life. The rich man will fade, beauty will be destroyed, and the scorching heat will wither the blossom. Don't miss this reality check.

I got a tune-up on my perspective one afternoon while playing "tree house" with my five-year-old buddy, Addison. Touting his favorite mug he bubbled, "Lookie here, Carlo. [He still uses that nickname he gave me.] I got to write my name on this cup. And I drawed this picture of the ship—it's a treasure ship with real pirates!"

"Cool!" I replied. "What else you got in this tree house?"

As he turned to show me his collection of rocks in the corner, he accidentally kicked his mug out of the tree house. Like firefighters on fire, we slid down the tree to assess the damage. Having landed on a rock, the mug looked more like a pile of powder.

"I'm sorry, Addison," I said. "I know how much you loved that mug."

Trying to place a couple of pieces together, he said, "Oh, that's OK—now it's a puzzle." Noticing how small the pieces were, he added, "A *very hard* puzzle!"

Now that's what I call good perspective in a trial. Our material possessions will be destroyed. There's no way around such trials, but don't lose perspective.

To punctuate his point about perspective, James then reminds us, "Blessed is the man who perseveres under trial, because when he has stood the test, he will receive the crown of life that God has promised to those who love him" (James 1:12).

James goes full circle in this passage and underscores his original point that we should consider it pure joy when we face trials. He reminds us: "Happy is the person who perseveres under trial, because someday he will receive a crown of life!"

A woman named Ardell comes to mind. She knows all about pain. She is a fifty-something invalid who lives in Minnesota and suffers twenty-four hours a day. Although there was a day when she was happily married with two sons, now she is alone and completely debilitated. A stroke left her sharp mind imprisoned in an unresponsive body.

Ardell lost full function of her legs and her right arm; she can barely budge her left arm. She cannot speak, and lifting her head is a tedious and complicated chore. The primary way that Ardell communicates is by turning her body to maneuver her left arm across a word board on her wheelchair. The word board contains 150 different words and phrases—expressions like "Thank you" and "Praise the Lord." There's one other way that Ardell communicates and that's with an electric typewriter. By placing her arm into a sling, she can move her finger over a key to press it.

Imagine this widow. She is all alone and entirely dependent on the caregivers at her nursing home to survive. Nevertheless, she lives in the hope of the hereafter. Listen to her testimony (which took two full days for her to type):

> God has blessed me throughout this ordeal. I'm so thankful too that the hardest part is over with. I can type with one finger and can feed myself. I have a word letter chart on the tray of my wheelchair. I can communicate by using that. All these things a normal person takes for

> granted. I am very thankful to God that I can do these things.
>
> Thank you God for life and glorifying your name with my experience. Give me strength and courage so I will glorify your name. I accept your will if it is to be healed. I am very thankful that in eternity we will have new and well bodies. In the name of Jesus we have this promise of eternal life. Amen.[7]

In our world of pain and trials, Ardell's testimony rings a reminder that there is a "crown of life that God has promised to those who love Him." Never lose that perspective. For someday you will be richly rewarded. There's no doubt about it.

3

James 1:13-18

Living Like Gilligan on Temptation Island

One of the most popular shows in recent years is Fox's blockbuster hit, *Temptation Island.* In its first season, the show dominated the TV Nielsen ratings among younger viewers. While I have not seen the show (although I was very tempted to watch it for research purposes!), the premise of the program is clear. Several unmarried couples travel to a Caribbean island to test their resolve to resist temptation. The couples are separated by gender and left for two weeks in the titillating company of thirty very attractive, scantily clad singles of the opposite sex. The point is to seduce one person in the couple, with the intent of possibly starting a new relationship.

Temptation Island is part of the exploding number of "reality" shows that offer unscripted smut for prime-time viewers (as though it's "reality" for half-naked people who look like Pamela Anderson to swoon over guys who spent their Saturday nights through high school playing video games by themselves). Columnist Chris Stevens of the *Daily News* offered this critique: "Just when you thought television programming had hit rock bottom, along comes a new show to test our evolving taste for garbage. Say hello to *Temptation Island*. . . . Fox calls it 'provocative' television, but it's more akin to cow dung."

Do you ever wonder what happened to programs like *Gilligan's Island*? Remember the days when the big scandal was exposing Ginger's belly button? Where the story lines centered on plots like Mr. Howell getting aced by Gilligan in a round of golf?

Let's face it. We don't live on Gilligan's Island any more. Instead, we devise an environment of evil in order to intensify the lure of temptation. This way, 12 million voyeurs can tune in on Wednesday evenings to watch.

I confess that I miss the polyester days on this one. While it may have been a bit corny and contrived, *Gilligan's Island* did have an aura of innocence to it. There was a hint of purity to the show—at least compared to *Temptation Island*.

So how do we recapture that innocence lost? How can we stay clean in a world so corrupt? How do we live like Gilligan in a world like Temptation Island?

To answer these questions is to set a course for spiritual growth. If you are serious about reflecting the character of Christ then you must master the art of tackling temptation. Unless you become a temptation management champion, you are destined to spiritual ruin. When you think about it, every person who has ever been destroyed spiritually has failed because of temptation. Therefore, to identify and resist temptation is a critical need for every follower of Christ.

Some years ago psychologists conducted an experiment that highlighted the importance of resisting temptation. It has now become known as the "marshmallow test." A four-year-old sits by a table with one marshmallow on it and is informed that the experimenter must leave temporarily. If the kid can wait for the experimenter to return, he will be rewarded with two marshmallows. If he opts to eat one right away, he can—but he doesn't get another one later.

The burning question at the heart of this research is "Can a four-year-old resist temptation?" If so, what are the benefits? If not, what are the consequences?

In the experiment, kids would develop all kinds of clever strategies to reinforce their resolve to resist the marshmallow—tell stories, sing songs, twiddle their fingers. One kid even tried to lick the table, as though the flavor had sunk into the wood!

As it turns out, there is a fascinating correlation between resisting temptation at the age of four and the outcome in the lives of the child participants. A Stanford University research team studied the kids for many years. Consider the final report:

> Those who were able to wait as four-year-olds grew up to be more socially competent, better able to cope with stress, and less likely to give up under pressure than those who could not wait. The marshmallow-grabbers grew up to be more stubborn and indecisive, more easily upset by frustration, and more resentful about not getting enough. Most amazingly, the group of marshmallow-waiters had SAT scores that averaged *210 points higher* than the group of marshmallow-grabbers!"[8]

So what's your marshmallow? Maybe it's a pint of Ben and Jerry's Chunky Monkey ice cream. Maybe it's a Game Boy. Maybe it comes in a bottle. Maybe it's a Web site. Maybe you smoke it. Maybe it's a critical spirit against other marshmallow eaters. Where are you most vulnerable to temptation?

In Scripture, the idea of temptation is allowing oneself to be torn away from God. In God's view, it is never a trivial thing. In our day, as we see on *Temptation Island,* the notion is often trivialized. In the Bible, when it comes to temptation, the human soul is at stake. Giving in to temptation means allowing myself to be separated from the God who loves me. And that's as bad as it gets. That's why it is imperative for you and me to get real clear on how we're going to triumph on Temptation Island.

Fortunately, James can help us with a strategy for surviving on Temptation Island. Get a load of his game plan.

1. Be realistic

The first survival strategy on Temptation Island is to be realistic about the inevitability of temptation. James begins his teaching on the topic by saying, "When tempted" (James 1:13). He does not say "*If* tempted." Rather, he assumes temptation. Being a Christian does not safeguard you from temptation. Christian or atheist, you will be tempted. Boy, girl, or Boy George—choose any of the three genders and you will be tempted.

Too often I fear that we become like the woman who was bathing in the Gulf of Mexico. While relaxing on an inflated cushion that kept her afloat, she failed to realize that the current had swept her about a mile from the beach. "Help!" she screamed. Of course, no one could hear her. Eventually, a coast guard craft found her five miles from the place where she first entered the water. She did not see her danger until she was beyond her own strength and ability.

Don't ever get complacent when it comes to temptation. Before you know it, you can drift into deeply ingrained patterns of sin. Everyone is vulnerable to being swept away when we get apathetic about the nature and power of temptation.

2. Be responsible

The second survival strategy for Temptation Island is to be responsible. James continues: "When tempted, no one should say, 'God is tempting me.' For God cannot be tempted by evil, nor does he tempt anyone" (James 1:13).

Oh, how we love to blame circumstances or Satan or someone else for our problems and moral lapses, don't we? James says, "Don't blame God. Don't blame the devil. The devil did not make you do it." You and I control our own destinies and we have to be responsible.

Some years ago (long before we had children of our own) I offered to baby-sit for some friends who had two boys, Bradley, age 5, and Skimmer, age 2. "Anytime you'd like to get away for the weekend," I said, "we'd be glad to take your kids." It made me feel real philanthropic to offer—until they took me up on it.

My wife, Cherié, had to work on the Friday they came by. I could tell she was apprehensive about me taking care of two kids. Over and over she asked, "Are you sure you'll be all right? Do you know the phone number for 9-1-1?"

"Of course." I was offended that she would question my competence at parenting. After all, I was raised by parents, wasn't I? "Trust me, Cherié, we'll be fine. I'm going to study, and the boys can watch me."

When their mom dropped off the kids she mentioned, "Ah, by the way, Skimmer won't eat vegetables."

Skimmer won't eat vegetables? I thought. *That's crazy! Two-year-olds don't have taste buds. Besides, since when do two-year-olds get to decide what they want to eat? Obviously, Skimmer's mom doesn't know how to persuade kids. Won't eat vegetables—ridiculous!*

At lunchtime, I served up some macaroni and cheese with a side of carrots. Both kids loved my macaroni and cheese. Bradley loved the carrots. Skimmer refused to touch the carrots.

"Skimmer," I said firmly, "please open up." Clenched fists; closed mouth.

"Skimmer." I amp-ed up the volume a notch. "If you want dessert, open up." Clenched fists; closed mouth.

"Skimmer," my voice rose in a crescendo that should have scared anything breathing, "if you ever want to eat again, open up!" Clenched fists; closed mouth.

Then I remembered Psychology 101. I looked Skimmer in the eyes and laughed. Strategically placing the carrots on the spoon, I cooed, "Loooookie here, Skimmer has an airplane. Oh no, the airplane needs to land. Now, open up the hanger!"

The garage door was closed.

In desperation, I said, "Fine, the airplane will crash right through the door."

And it did. I smeared and smashed carrots right in his mouth!

He sat motionless. His face turned red. Skimmer would rather croak than swallow carrots.

Are you familiar with the law of thermodynamics? It postulates that if you hold your thumb over a hose and increase the water pressure, eventually the water will burst out with greater force than with which it went in.

In other words, Mount Saint Skimmer erupted.

Carrots coated the dining room. And the kitchen. And the bedroom. There were carrots everywhere—except in Skimmer.

Later, when Cherié came home she asked about the "orange gunk in the vent."

"Oh, you mean the carrots? Um, well, . . . Skimmer won't eat vegetables."

At two years old, Skimmer understood that he directed his own destiny. If he didn't want to eat carrots, he was not going to eat carrots. Period! Only he would choose his destiny.

Skimmer understood that principle better than some adults do. We tend to rationalize everything. It's always somebody else's fault.

"But you don't understand what he did to me."

"I'm hopelessly addicted to pornography. It's my dad's fault for exposing me at an early age."

"My boss is putting me under so much pressure, I've got to get a drink."

"She's impossible to live with. She's the cause of my anger."

Not true! You are responsible. Whatever the marshmallow in your life, you are the only one who can spit it out.

3. Be ready

The third survival strategy for Temptation Island is to be ready. Notice verses 14 and 15: "But each one is tempted when, by his own evil desire, he is dragged away and enticed. Then, after desire has conceived, it gives birth to sin; and sin, when it is full-grown, gives birth to death."

James is tipping us off to a predictable pattern of temptation so that we can be ready to meet it. Temptation begins with an *"evil desire."* This is the initial point of involvement—when you begin to entertain the thought. What if I had a fling? Who would know if I took the money? Why not share some gossip? Temptation always starts with an evil desire.

Next comes the deception when "He is dragged away and enticed." The Greek word, *exelko,* is translated "dragged away." The word suggests persuasion. It's from the same word that Jesus used when He said, " 'But I, when I am lifted up from the earth, will draw all men to myself' " (John 12:32). The word suggests a wooing. James also borrows a word from the fisherman's vocabulary, translated "enticed," which means to lure by bait. While I'm not a fisherman, I understand that it's a real art. I once heard a fisherman say, "The next thing to a genius is a bass." But no matter how many fishermen you talk to, they all say that the secret to fishing is using the right bait for the right fish. Similarly, Satan is a master at hooking you and me. He knows the right kind of bait to use for every believer. But beware, the bait always looks better than it really is.

Finally, when temptation runs its full course, the desire and deception result in death. "Then, after desire has conceived, it gives birth to sin; and sin, when it is full-grown, gives birth to death. Don't be deceived, my dear brothers. Every good and perfect gift is from above, coming down from the Father of the heavenly lights, who does not change like shifting shadows" (James 1:15-17).

Sure the marshmallow looks good. But it is poison packaged in sugar. Only God the Father is the Author of what is good. Go after Satan's bait and it will destroy your soul.

Cindy Cohen's story comes to mind. She was not the type to feast on Satan's bait. She just felt trapped in her job as senior accountant at a large commercial bank in Manhattan.

So to break her monotony, Cindy responded to an advertisement in *Travel and Leisure* magazine, offering a winter special at the Club Med in Martinique. It turned out to be her dream retreat that resulted in a nightmare.

At first Cindy felt out of place at the Caribbean resort, her pale complexion made whiter by number 21 sun block. Then she hooked up with three dynamos from Dallas—bottle blondes with bronzed skin, long slender fingers that ended in red press-on nails, and lean figures for women in their 40s with kids.

Cindy tagged along with the trio from Texas on a snorkeling trip guided by Frederic, a diver from Nice who spent each winter working at Club Med Martinique.

Frederic charmed Cindy in a way that made her feel young and desirable. Although this was out of character for her, Cindy succumbed to a romantic fling. Over the next four days, she and Frederic stole away several times to make love.

About a week after Cindy returned to New York City, she came down with what seemed like the flu. Glands in her neck swelled, her muscles ached, and she had a viselike headache and a fever of 103 degrees. Later Cindy discovered that she had HIV, the virus that causes AIDS.

Immediately Cindy visited Dr. Jerome Groopman, chief of experimental medicine at Beth Israel Deaconess Medical Center and one of the world's leading AIDS researchers. In his book, *The Measure of Our Days,* Dr. Groopman tells Cindy's story. He says that while treating her, he wondered: *Is AIDS really unstoppable? Isn't HIV just a puny parasite, nothing more than eleven genes in a feeble protein shell?*

While it may be just a puny parasite, it can still destroy. Such was the case for Cindy. In her words, "There are moments when I feel so alone, so afraid. I go to work, talk with my mother, see a movie with a girlfriend. But behind me is this huge leering monster, a horrible thing with fangs and sharp claws. It's always stalking me."[9]

I read Cindy's story while on a flight across the country. I found her tragedy heart wrenching, and I couldn't mask my emotions.

Noticing my tears, the passenger next to me asked, "Um, sir, are you all right?"

"Ah, I'm, ah, fine," I managed to answer.

"Frankly," she said, "it's nice to see a grown man cry. My husband never cries. But may I ask why you're upset?"

I shared Cindy's story then said, "If only people would think about the consequences of sin before they bite on temptation."

"I couldn't agree more," the woman replied. "I have always believed that choosing any path other than purity can wreck a soul."

Her observation is still embedded in my mind. She shared a priceless gem of advice that's worth filing away for the next time you're tempted. Scoff at the counsel of Scripture on this one and you're playing Russian roulette with your soul.

So be ready when temptation comes whispering. Desire, deception, then death—it's a path of pain. Don't go there.

4. Be reborn

The final survival tip for Temptation Island is to be reborn. "He chose to give us birth through the word of truth, that we might be a kind of firstfruits of all he created" (James 1:18). Notice that it is God who acts in order to give us birth.

Bruce Larson, pastor of the University Presbyterian Church in Seattle, tells the story of an old priest who was asked by a young man, "Father, when will I cease to be bothered by the temptations of the flesh?"

The priest replied, "I wouldn't trust myself, Son, until I was dead for three days."

The bottom line is you can't trust yourself to conquer temptation. You can't lick temptation until you have been reborn. Only in God's power will you have access to the strength to live right on Temptation Island.

The best way to avoid eating a marshmallow is not by trying really hard; the best way is to make sure that you are eating better stuff on a regular basis. You will always be eating something, and if you don't eat the good stuff you'll eat the junk.

Look at the Master of temptation management. The tempter comes to Jesus in the wilderness. After every temptation Jesus answers with the words, "It is written . . ." Jesus was so washed in the Word that He lived in its reality. In the same manner, James calls us to be reborn through the Word of truth. In anchoring our lives in Scripture, we fortify our souls against the tempter.

So identify your marshmallow—where you are most likely to be tempted—then immerse your mind in relevant Scripture. If anger is your marshmallow, then you should camp in verses like Ecclesiastes 7:9: "Do not be quickly provoked in your spirit, for anger resides in the lap of fools." Recite the verse over and over then practice it.

If your marshmallow is lust, look at verses like 1 John 2:16, 17: "For everything in the world—the cravings of sinful man, the lust of his eyes and the boasting of what he has and does—comes not from the Father but from the world. The world and its desires pass away, but the man who does the will of God lives forever." When tempted to nurture prurient thoughts, focus instead on the promises of God's Word.

If your marshmallow is a grumbling spirit, then live with 1Thessalonians 5:18 in your heart: "Give thanks in all circumstances, for this is God's will for you in Christ Jesus." Say it over and over, "Give thanks," and then practice it.

Perhaps you feel as though you have established permanent residency on Temptation Island. Maybe your battle is not going so well and you feel helpless to move off the island. Maybe you are wondering right now, *Is there enough grace for me? Is it hopeless? Will I ever be rescued from this island?*

For you I offer a well-worn prayer. Parents still use it to protect their kids at night. It's a sober prayer: "Now I lay me down to sleep,

I pray Thee, Lord, my soul to keep. If I should die before I wake, I pray Thee, Lord, my soul to take."

The second verse gets a little darker. "Our days begin with trouble here, our life is but a span, and cruel death is always near, so frail a thing as man."

How's that for a cheery postlude to tuck in Junior at night? "Don't let the bed bugs bite . . . cruel death is always near . . . good night, honey."

Why has the prayer proven to be so timeless? Because life is a battle, and we are quite frail. We have an enemy. Our one hope is to pray for God our souls to keep. Your soul is at stake and your soul is precious to God. So no matter how often you have fallen, you can get back up. God will help you. It is worth the struggle.

We have an enemy who is strong. But there is One who is stronger still. He has won the battle. Whatever your temptation, you don't face it alone. So make this your prayer. Pray for the protection of your soul from the destruction and death of temptation. And claim victory, for Jesus has won the battle!

You do not have to die on Temptation Island. There is a cross that bridges lost humanity, stranded on an island of sin and temptation, to the throne room of heaven, where the Son of man covers you in His righteousness. You really can live a life of holiness—even on Temptation Island.

James 1:19-21

Relationships 101

What can I say about relationships?

Nothing.

See, that's the problem. Guys don't have a clue about relationships and the expression of their deep, innermost feelings. In fact, scientists have questioned whether guys *have* deep, innermost feelings—unless you count their passion for the Green Bay Packers or the belching contest at a bachelor party.

Women, on the other hand, they *get* relationships. They have deep, innermost feelings where guys can't even scratch. I submit for your consideration this case study.

Bob and Brenda have been going out for three months. Then one evening after seeing the *Nutcracker* ballet, Brenda says, "That was a wonderful version of the *Nutcracker*! I love how we share special moments like this in our relationship."

That's when Brenda panics. She thinks, *Oh, no! I shouldn't have said anything so forward. I used the word* relationship. *Maybe relationships scare him. Like a relationship is too confining. Perhaps he's confused by his feelings for me.*

Meanwhile, Bob is thinking: *Nutcracker.*

And Brenda thinks, *Maybe our relationship is going too fast. I have feelings for Bob, but if his feelings for me aren't the same, maybe I need to back off.*

And Bob thinks, *Nutcracker—that's what I can get Aunt Mabel for Christmas. She loves nuts. And I've never seen a nutcracker in her kitchen.*

So Bob says, "Yeah, that's a good idea."

And Brenda thinks, *What's a good idea? That we share moments like the Nutcracker more often? Or that we simmer our feelings for each other? Bob is such a deep thinker; I just can't read him.*

And Bob thinks, *What does a nutcracker cost? Maybe three bucks? Does Wal-Mart sell them?*

And Brenda thinks, *He's not saying anything. He's mad. I was so stupid!*

So she cautiously asks, "Bob, do you really feel that way?"

"What way?" Bob asks. Then he opts for what he thinks is the right answer. "Yes."

Finally, Bob pulls into Brenda's driveway and says curtly, "Good night." He's hoping Wal-Mart is still open.

Brenda retreats to her bedroom and spends the rest of the evening torturing herself with feelings.

OK, maybe my case study is an exaggeration. I admit, you can't really get a nutcracker for three bucks, even at Wal-Mart.

But the rest of the case study is true. Relationships can be tough. Intimacy can be tricky. Communication is not easy. (At least that's how I *feel* about it!)

That's why we ought to master the relationship fundamentals that James offers. Any experienced coach will tell you that success begins with mastering the basics. Back in the glory years of the Green Bay Packers, Vince Lombardi was known to line everybody up after a lackluster game, hold up the pigskin and say, "Gentlemen, this is a football." John Wooden, the legendary basketball coach of the UCLA Bruins, used to devote the first practice of the year to teaching players how to put on their socks. He did this to prevent blisters that might sideline a player for a key game. In the sporting world, fundamentals are key.

Fundamentals are equally important in the world of relationships. Just imagine the benefits if you ace this course. For example, researcher William Menninger found that when people lose their jobs, 80 percent of the time it's not for technical incompetence. Rather, it's because they can't get along with people. So if you master the fundamentals of relationships, the likelihood of success in the workplace increases.

Dr. James Lynch found that isolated people live significantly shorter lives. If you master the fundamentals you're likely to live longer.

The *Adventist Review* published the results of a survey, which concluded the number one reason that people leave the Seventh-day Adventist Church was not doctrinal disagreements but rather relational conflicts. So if you master the fundamentals, the likelihood of having a positive experience in church increases as well.

Daniel Goleman, in his book, *Emotional Intelligence,* cites one study that documents the increasing chances of divorce in our day. According to this study, a couple that got married in the 1950s had a 30 percent chance of divorce. A couple married in the 1990s faced a 67 percent chance of divorce. Research suggests that one of the primary reasons for divorce is communication. Sadly, it doesn't appear that we're improving at it. If only people would practice relationship fundamentals.

In sum, practice these fundamentals and some of the benefits you'll enjoy include:

- Greater job satisfaction
- Increased life longevity
- Harmonious church experience
- Improved marriage

Now let's open the textbook. Pay attention—the relationship you save just might be your own.

"My dear brothers, take note of this: Everyone should be quick to listen, slow to speak and slow to become angry, for man's anger does not bring about the righteous life that God desires" (James 1:19, 20).

James's advice is so simple. If only we would put it into practice.

Some businesses have discovered the wisdom in James's words. For example, consider the case study of a very successful grocery store in Connecticut. Stu Leonard's grocery store grossed over $100 million last year. To put this number in perspective, check out this fact. The average grocery store makes $300 per square foot. But Stu's store makes $3,000 per square foot!

Here's another amazing fact. The average grocery store stocks 15,000 items, but Stu stocks only 700.

What's going on? Stu Leonard profits from putting James 1:19, 20 into practice.

Picture this actual scene. While walking the aisles of his store, Stu stops to ask a customer how she likes the fresh fish. She responds, "I don't think it's fresh."

Stu explains how the fish is brought in from the Boston pier every morning and that it is the freshest fish money can buy. Again, she comments, "I don't think it's fresh."

So Stu calls Nick, the head of the seafood department, to hear the complaint. Stu asks Nick if their fish is fresh. Nick makes a major speech about bringing in the fish from the Boston pier every morning. Then they both look at the woman and ask: "What do you think of our fresh fish?"

She says, "I still don't think the fish is fresh."

At this point most of us would probably say something like, "Look, lady, we'll put you on the truck, drive you to the Boston pier, and prove that we're right and you're wrong!"

But Stu Leonard doesn't do that. Instead, he asks her more questions. "What exactly do you mean—our fish isn't fresh?"

"Look at it," she replies. "You have that filet sitting on a green cardboard container. You have plastic wrap over the filet—and it's wrinkled. And you have a price sticker over the other half of the filet so I can't even see it. You must be trying to hide something."

Then Stu patiently asks, "What would fresh fish look like to you?"

"I go to Boston all the time," she said, "and I like to see the fish on ice."

Stu listens.

In fact, after this actual conversation Stu walked across the aisle and laid his fresh fish on ice. His fish sales soared from 15,000 pounds a week to 30,000 pounds a week—and stayed there!

Following James's counsel can result in significant opportunities for us. James outlines a simple strategy that informs us how we too can profit from Stu's technique. It's as simple as 1-2-3.

1. Be quick to listen

Nothing nourishes relationships better than genuine listening. Want to express love to another human being? Try listening. It is the universal love language of every human spirit.

When I first got married, I tried to speak Cherié's love language via flowers. Assuming that every woman loves flowers, I arrived home from class one evening with a couple dozen long-stemmed beauties.

"Wow! Thanks," she said, "but how much did they cost? They're beautiful, but shouldn't we be paying off our school bill or getting tires for the car? Honey, you really don't need to go extravagant on the flowers."

Message received. I discovered that Cherié's love language isn't that expensive. While Cherié likes flowers, she likes it even more when I just listen. It's that simple—but it's not easy. Occasionally Cherié will launch into a monologue that waxes on and on and on. On the outside I'm listening, but on the inside I'm thinking about how I could have improved my golf score had I not three-putted the last four greens. Then Cherié will land on that dreaded question: "I don't know, what do you think?"

I scramble for the rewind button. "Well, um, that's a tough one. What do you think?"

Whether it's your spouse, your teacher, your roommate, your basketball teammates, your siblings, your kids, or your mailman—listening will dramatically improve any relationship.

Open the photo album of Jesus' life and it's chock-full of snapshots of Him listening. Notice the three things He did that distinguished Him as a world-class listener.

First, Jesus looked at people. World-class listeners focus on you when you talk. Ever talk with someone whose eyes are dancing about the room looking for whom they'll talk to next?

Not Jesus. He paid attention. Look at the Gospel of John, chapter 9, where Jesus encounters a blind man. John keeps playing with this word "see," because Jesus could see as no other human being on earth. Jesus healed the blind man that others never saw. Imagine the scene:

> Having said this, [Jesus] spit on the ground, made some mud with the saliva, and put it on the man's eyes. "Go," he told him, "wash in the Pool of Siloam" (this word means Sent). So the man went and washed, and came home seeing.
>
> His neighbors and those who had formerly seen him begging asked, "Isn't this the same man who used to sit and beg?" Some claimed that he was.
>
> Others said, "No, he only looks like him."
>
> But he himself insisted, "I am the man."
>
> "How then were your eyes opened?" they demanded.

> He replied, "The man they call Jesus made some mud and put it on my eyes. He told me to go to Siloam and wash. So I went and washed, and then I could see" (John 9:6-11).

This blind man had been a permanent fixture in the neighborhood for thirty, maybe forty years, but nobody noticed him. Nobody stopped to *look* at him. Everyone overlooked him except Jesus. Jesus saw beyond the blindness and beheld a beloved child.

Now imagine developing the eyes of Jesus. When is the last time you really looked at somebody—a friend, your spouse, maybe a child—full in the face, and you *saw* them? You noticed what makes their eyes dance, their shoulders sag, or their spirit soar.

Second, Jesus asked questions. "Where is your husband?" he asks the Samaritan woman. "Do you want to get well?" he asks the invalid of thirty-eight years. "What were you arguing about?" "Which of these three do you think was a neighbor to the man?" "Do you truly love Me more than these?"

Over and over, Jesus would ask questions of Roman army officers, rabbis, prostitutes, disciples, politicians, mothers, and lawyers. Then He would stop to listen. He was genuinely interested in what people would say. It's hard to imagine, isn't it? Here was God Himself, the Answer Incarnate to all questions, yet He humbled Himself enough to ask.

Max Lucado captures it this way:

> I think it's noteworthy that the Almighty didn't act high and mighty. The Holy One wasn't holier-than-thou. The One who knew it all wasn't a know-it-all. The One who made the stars didn't keep his head in them. The One who owns all the stuff of earth never strutted it.
>
> Never. He could have. Oh, how he could have!

> He could have been a name-dropper: "*Did I ever tell you of the time Moses and I went up on the mountain?*"
>
> He could have been a showoff: "*Hey, want me to beam you into the twentieth century?*"
>
> He could have been a smart-aleck: "*I know what you're thinking. Want me to prove it?*"
>
> He could have been highbrow and uppity: "*I've got some property on Jupiter . . .*"
>
> Jesus could have been all of these, but he wasn't. His purpose was not to show off but to show up.[10]

You too can develop the ears of Jesus. If you want to be a world-class listener, just ask questions: How are you doing? What gives you joy? What are you learning these days? What are your dreams? How's your soul?

Then listen. *Really* listen.

Thirdly, Jesus touched people. The final mark of a world-class listener is that they offer appropriate touch. They know that sometimes a hand on the shoulder or a simple hug can communicate far more love than words ever can.

The importance of touching was studied as far back as the thirteenth century. The German emperor, Frederick II, conducted an appalling experiment to find out what language kids would speak if they were raised without hearing anybody talking. He took several newborns from their parents and put them in the custody of nurses who had been instructed never to touch or talk with them. These babies never learned a language because they died before they could talk. In the year 1248, the historian Salimbene commented on the babies: "They could not live without petting."

In the face of more recent studies documenting the importance of human touch, we still do not touch very much in the United States. Psychologist Sidney Jourard reported how many times couples in cafés casually touched each other in an hour. The highest rates were in Puerto Rico, at 180 times per hour. In the United States couples touched only twice. In London, it was *zero!* [11] They never touched. Because I come from a long line of English ancestors, I know that we tend to insist on having conversations in separate rooms so that no accidental touching occurs. This is unfortunate because every human spirit craves meaningful touch.

Again, Jesus was the master of this. One time a leper approached Jesus and cried out, " 'Lord, if you are willing, you can make me clean' " (Matthew 8:2). It was against the law for Jesus to talk to the leper, let alone touch him. Before the healing, however, Jesus does an extraordinary thing. Rather than simply declaring the man to be whole, first He reaches down and touches the leper.

Why did Jesus do that? Clearly Jesus understood the power of touch. Max Lucado offers this challenge:

> Oh, the power of a godly touch. Haven't you known it? The doctor who treated you, or the teacher who dried your tears? Was there a hand holding yours at a funeral? Another on your shoulder during a trial? A handshake of welcome at a new job? A pastoral prayer for healing? Haven't we known the power of a godly touch?
>
> Can't we offer the same?
>
> Many of you already do. Some of you have the master touch of the Physician himself. You use your hands to pray over the sick and minister to the weak. If you aren't touching them personally, your hands are writing letters, dialing phones, baking pies. You have learned the power of a touch.
>
> But others of us tend to forget. Our hearts are good; it's just that our memories are bad. We forget how significant

one touch can be. We fear saying the wrong thing or using the wrong tone or acting the wrong way. So rather than do it incorrectly, we do nothing at all.

Aren't we glad Jesus didn't make the same mistake? If your fear of doing the wrong thing prevents you from doing anything, keep in mind the perspective of the lepers of the world. They aren't picky. They aren't finicky. They're just lonely. They are yearning for a godly touch.

Jesus touched the untouchables of the world. Will you do the same?[12]

So be quick to listen. How? Look. Ask. Touch.

2. Be slow to speak

On our globe of gabbers, it is a rare person who carefully weighs his or her words before talking.

Pastor John Ortberg tells this story:

> One afternoon my family waited in a sitting room for my sister to come up from her dorm to join us for Family Day. In the same room was a mother of a classmate of my sister, who was waiting with her eight-year-old son. For an hour and fifteen minutes we waited, and I don't suppose that woman stopped talking longer than it took to inhale. She talked—as the saying went before the day of compact discs—as if she'd been vaccinated with a phonograph needle. She talked as if words were the rope that kept her tethered to the earth. She talked until I knew more about her family than I did about some of my closest relatives.
>
> Finally her daughter stepped into the room. "Well, we must be going," said the mom, keeping the torrent flowing. "I have to get reservations for dinner. We have to meet my husband at the restaurant, you know, and oh, yes, I need to stop by the store and get some buttons."

> Then her son spoke. The only words, as best I can recollect it, that he uttered during the whole hour and fifteen minutes. He turned to his mother and said as only an eight-year-old could: "Mother, you need a button for your mouth."
>
> Out of the mouths of babes.[13]

Not a bad idea, eh? Numerous are the occasions when I wish I had had a button for my mouth. Don't you know people that you'd love to give a gift button next Christmas? So often we sabotage our relationships by speaking too much.

Frederick Buechner describes a character that talked too much: "Words came spilling out of him. He didn't even care what he talked about. He'd rattle on till the spittle gathered at the corners of his mouth, and if you made a move to leave, there would come to his eyes a haunted look and he would talk all the faster to try to force you to stay."

You may know people like that. They feel lonely, and the more lonely they feel the more they talk, and the more they talk, the more it drives away potential friends. And the cycle continues. The more people move away, the more lonely they feel, and so they talk all the more. The irony of it is that talking too much is an attempt to connect with people, but it ends up driving them away.

All of us would enjoy deeper intimacy if we could master this principle: Be slow to speak. This is the basic stuff of relationships. Be quick to listen, slow to speak, and finally, be slow to anger.

3. Be slow to anger.

James Dobson tells of a family on vacation. As the miles mounted so did the father's fury. For days the two sons bickered, whined, griped, grumbled, and fussed.

Finally the father's fuse was finished. Jerking the car over to the side of the road, the father yanked both boys outside. "I can't take it any longer!" he screamed in anger. After spanking them both, he shoved them back into the car with a stern warning: "If I hear a peep from either of you for thirty minutes I'll give you some more of what you just had."

The boys got the message. They sat mute and motionless.

Exactly thirty minutes later—to the very second—the older brother peeped, "Is it OK to talk now?"

The father barked, "What do you need to say?"

"Well, when you spanked us back there, my shoe fell off."

When you let anger fly, shoes have a way of falling off. Unchecked anger inevitably boomerangs to bite you.

Jim Taylor in *Currents* tells the following story about his friend, Ralph Milton. One morning Ralph woke up at five o'clock to a noise that sounded like someone repairing boilers on his roof. Still in his pajamas, he went into the backyard to investigate. He found a woodpecker on the TV antenna, "pounding its little brains out on the metal pole." Angry at the little creature that ruined his sleep, Ralph picked up a rock and threw it. The rock sailed over the house—shattering the windshield of his car. In utter disgust, Ralph took a vicious kick at a clod of dirt, only to remember—too late—that he was still in his bare feet. Uncontrolled anger, as Ralph learned, can sometimes be its own reward.[14]

Furthermore, angry people die young. Men who score high for hostility on standard tests are four times more likely to die prematurely than men whose scores are low.[15]

The bottom line is simple: Anger will wreck your relationships. You can do life like an angry geyser that spouts regularly, but the person most damaged is yourself. So remind yourself that life is too short and intimacy is too precious for you to wreck your relationships with rage.

Practice James's anger management nugget today. Say to yourself, "When I get angry, I'm not going to just flip into my default mode. I'll think before I respond. If I tend to blow up, I'll pause and respond calmly. If I tend to avoid needed confrontation, I will swallow deep and have the courage to speak the truth in love. I will be slow to anger."

Research informs us that reading, by itself, results in one of the lowest levels of learning. Perusing this chapter nets you about 5 percent of the information. On the other end of the spectrum, the highest level of learning occurs when you assimilate the knowledge by practicing it. When you put the principles into practice, you retain a stunning 95 percent of the material!

So what are you waiting for? If you really want to benefit from this crash course on relationships, go practice! Be quick to listen. Be slow to speak. And be slow to anger.

5

James 1:22-27

Mirror, Mirror in the Word

Technology hates me. I am sure the official time of my death will be 12:00 o'clock, because when the coroner comes to get my body that's the time that will be flashing on the VCR that I never learned to program. Again this morning I was reminded of technology's conspiracy against me. In trying to set up a computer and projector for a presentation, the timesaving technological marvels nicked me for the better part of an hour. I plugged, pried, probed, and prayed—all with no results. Meanwhile, several people offered unsolicited advice. Finally the chairman of the board said to the "expert" consultants, "I'll trade ten of you telling him what to do for one who will just go do it."

His jab brought to mind the words of James, "Do not merely listen to the word, and so deceive yourselves. Do what it says" (James 1:22). Henrik Ibsen once observed, "A thousand words will not leave so deep an impression as one deed."

Of what value is it to just hear the Word of God? James calls us to do it! Without action, it's like getting wise advice from a leading authority on a vitally important topic but never acting on the counsel. For example, suppose the elders of my church are concerned about my health, so they give me *The New Encyclopedia of Modern Bodybuilding* by Arnold Schwarzenegger.

A couple months later they ask me how it's going. "Terrific," I say, beaming. "It's a great book. I've studied it thoroughly. I arise early every morning and read passages of it. I've committed chunks of it to memory. I believe it's true. I even meet together with a group of guys on Tuesday mornings and we talk about the book over eggs and waffles and doughnuts and Cinnabons."

They ask, "But are you doing it?"

"Huh?"

"Are you doing what the book says?" they persist. "Are you doing the exercises and lifting the weights and letting it shape your activities?"

"Obviously not. Doing what the book says would require time, sweat, change, and pain. I'm all for it and I believe what it says, but I don't actually do it."

Similarly, God has entrusted to us His Word. The purpose of the Book is to usher us into life in the kingdom. Unless the Bible changes the way we live, it is of little value. That is, if you miss the transforming power of the Word, you miss the whole adventure.

Consider the haunting words of an anonymous author:

> I was hungry, and you formed a humanities club and discussed my hunger.
>
> I was imprisoned, and you crept off quietly to your chapel and prayed for my release.
>
> I was naked, and in your mind you debated the morality of my appearance.
>
> I was sick, and you knelt and thanked God for your health.
>
> I was homeless, and you preached to me of the spiritual shelter of the love of God.
>
> I was lonely, and you left me alone so you could pray for me.

> You seem so close to God; but I am still very hungry, and lonely, and cold.

James insists that it is possible to hear the Word and yet be deceived into thinking that we are actually doing what it says. James even uses a comical analogy to show our capacity for self-deception. He says it's like someone who looks in the mirror and then forgets what he looks like.

> Anyone who listens to the word but does not do what it says is like a man who looks at his face in a mirror and, after looking at himself, goes away and immediately forgets what he looks like. But the man who looks intently into the perfect law that gives freedom, and continues to do this, not forgetting what he has heard, but doing it—he will be blessed in what he does (James 1:23-25).

The human capacity for deception is frightening. Take, for example, our tendency to deceive ourselves when we look in the mirror. The words of Dave Barry come to mind:

> I sincerely believe that women are wiser than men are, with the exception of one key area, and that area is clothing sizes. In this particular area women are self-deceived. When a man shops for clothes his primary objective—follow me closely here—is to purchase clothes that fit on his particular body. A man will try a pair of pants and if those pants are too small he'll try a larger pair. When he finds a pair that fits he buys them. Most men do not spend a lot of time fretting about the size of their pants. Many men wear jeans with the size printed right on the back label so that if you're standing behind a man in the supermarket line you can read his waist and inseam size. A man could have a 52-inch waist and a 30-inch

> inseam and his label will proudly display this information. Which is basically the same thing as having a size that says, "Howdy, my caboose is the size of a Federal Express truck."
>
> The situation is very different with women. When a woman shops for clothes, her primary objective is not to find clothes that fit her particular body. She would like for that to be the case, but her primary objective is to purchase clothes that are the size she wore when she was 19 years old. This will be some arbitrary number such as 8, don't ask me 8 of what. That question has baffled scientists for centuries. She'll keep trying size 8 items on and unless they start fitting her, she'll become extremely unhappy.
>
> She may take this unhappiness out on her husband. "Am I fat?" she asks. This is a very bad situation for the man. Because if he answers "Yes" she'll be angry that he's saying she's fat. And if he answers "No" she'll be angry because he's obviously lying because none of the size 8s fit her.[16]

Dave Barry concludes that his wife doesn't really care if her clothes fit so long as they have the right number on them. He then suggests a sure-fire way to get rich—start a woman's clothing store called Size 2, in which all garments (including those that were originally intended to be restaurant awnings) have labels of size 2.

I suppose it only makes sense for marketers to cash in on our capacity for self-deception. We can deceive ourselves about how we look physically. James suggests that we can deceive ourselves spiritually as well.

It happens like this. I hear the Word. I agree with it. I affirm it in my heart. But I don't do anything about it.

So let's look in the mirror of God's Word. We'll see three body parts reflected that could easily deceive us.

First, look at the tongue. James writes, "If anyone considers himself religious and yet does not keep a tight rein on his tongue, he deceives himself and his religion is worthless" (James 1:26).

It's easy to hear and read the Word of God. We resonate with the wisdom of statements such as "Be quick to listen and slow to speak." But then we engage in malicious gossip or hateful criticism.

Arthur J. Snider offers a good illustration of the damage a tongue can do. Writing in the *Chicago Daily News,* he claims the average person can see a dot as small as eight-thousandths of an inch in diameter. But this is about 14,000 times larger than the smallest known virus.

Yet these microbes are the cause of at least 500 human diseases, some of which are very serious and can be fatal. One strain was responsible for the greatest pestilence civilization has ever experienced—the flu epidemic of 1918-1919. That scourge claimed more lives than World War I.

The Bible warns of another small thing that can inflict great harm. It's that "little member" known as the tongue. James would probably suggest that the most effective vaccine to bring its deadly effects under control is the Word of God. That's assuming that we do the Word, rather than simply read it.

Recently I saw the deadly potential of the tongue. Several years ago a travel troupe visited our campus at Walla Walla College to conduct a Week of Prayer. For whatever reason, many people judged their programs to be "irrelevant" and "childish." Such opinions were amply expressed in the school newspaper. Petitions calling for a boycott of the meetings circulated freely.

Eight months later I was speaking at a convention on the East Coast. Ironically, this same group was performing in the youth department.

Bumping into a member of the team, I initiated a conversation. "Hi, I'm Karl Haffner, from Walla Walla College Church."

Almost instantaneously the young woman burst like a pipe. Through the tears she shared her story. "I know who you are," she said. "Some friends recommended that I attend your evening meetings, but I haven't mustered the courage yet. Being reminded of Walla Walla College is still too painful. That was our first Week of Prayer on a college campus and we knew our material wasn't connecting, but the harder we tried the worse it got." She went on to quote verbatim some of the hateful jabs that were published in the school paper. She recalled the cutting comments and venomous glances. Then she concluded, "That week was the darkest chapter of my life."

I ached for this young woman. To see her—eight months after the fact—break down at the thought of our college was a stinging indictment. It struck me how un-Christian it is to spew hurtful words. It takes no courage to fire off a hateful letter or make caustic comments. We can spit poison all over the place and carry on with no responsibility or remorse; meanwhile, the victim bleeds for months, even years.

James would call into question the Christianity of any community of faith that slanders people in that way. No wonder he says to examine your tongue in the mirror of God's Word.

So how about it? Can we just declare a moratorium on gossip, slander, and criticism? Can we tighten the reins on our tongues?

According to James, if we cannot do this, we have no right to call ourselves a Christian community. We're just deceiving ourselves, and our religion is worthless. Truth is, we are a community of brokenness, so let's acknowledge that and speak only words of grace.

Next, James counsels us to use Scripture to examine our hands. "Religion that God our Father accepts as pure and faultless is this: to look after orphans and widows in their distress" (James 1:27).

Pure and faultless religion is hands-on. That is, devoted followers of Christ do not merely talk about what they believe; they serve and take care of people in need. Louise Hannah Kohr offers this parable to illustrate:

Along a rugged coast in a far country the roads were marked with crosses. They etched themselves against the murky sky to guide the wayfarer aright.

Each day a traveler made his way over one of these roadways on the errands of life. Always he would turn at a weather-beaten cross. And many others passed that way.

One day as the man came over the brow of a nearby hill, he saw that a storm of the night had felled the cross. He passed by, but something would not let him go on. For how, he asked himself, would a stranger know the turn if the cross was fallen? He tried to brace the broken beam with a stone, but it would not stand. At last he gave up his journey and stayed to hold up the cross.

Another man who had passed that way for many days paused when he saw the man who upheld the cross. He asked why the man tended it. And the man answered, "It has stood for years marking the way. How could the stranger find his direction if it be fallen?"

The other man was greatly surprised, and his eyes were opened. For during all those days that he had passed that way, he had never noticed the cross until he saw it upheld by human hands.[17]

God's Word is like a mirror reflecting the genuineness of our faith. As you look into this mirror, what do you see when you observe your tongue? How about your hands?

Finally, consider the heart.

Note the punch line of verse 27. "Religion that God our Father accepts as pure and faultless is this: . . . to keep oneself from being polluted by the world."

Authentic religion tenaciously guards the heart in order to protect it from being polluted by the world. It flows out of a heart that is thoroughly possessed by God and not polluted by the world.

Some years ago, musicians noted that errand boys in a certain part of London all whistled out of tune as they went about their work. It was talked about and someone suggested that it was because the bells of Westminster were slightly out of tune. Something had gone wrong with the chimes and they were discordant. The boys did not know there was anything wrong with the peals, and quite unconsciously they had copied their pitch.

So it is that we tend to copy whatever we are exposed to; we become the books we read and the programs we watch and the discussions we have—almost without knowing it. That's why God has given us His Word, which is the perfect pitch for life. When we tune our hearts to it, we can then detect the false music of the world. Doing, then, flows out of the heart.

An old man stumbled into church just as the preacher was finishing his sermon. He asked the usher, "Is the sermon done yet?"

The usher replied, "The sermon has been preached; it has yet to be done."

James has preached us a sermon. But now it needs to be done. So call a friend who is battling cancer. Drop a note of encouragement to your kid's teacher. Volunteer at a soup kitchen. Weed a widow's garden. Baby-sit your neighbor's kid. Send $100 anonymously to someone who is struggling to make ends meet. Be a big brother. Hang out in a nursing home.

Whatever you do, use God's Word as a mirror to examine yourself. Do you see hands that hug the disenfranchised? A tongue that speaks words of compassion? A heart that beats to the cadence of Christ? If not, then you are Christian in name only. And in the final analysis, I'll trade ten Christians who read the Word for one who does the Word.

James 2:1-13

Country-Club Christianity

Someday when I'm so rich that Bill Gates hits me up for a loan, I'm going to buy a thousand acres of land. Then I'll hire some groundskeepers to follow me as I whack a golf ball 72 times. The gardeners behind me will be charged with the task of building a golf course around my errant shots. I figure that's the only way I will ever hit a round of par golf. With my severe slice, I reckon the course would be a perfect circle.

My stubborn slice notwithstanding, I am obsessive about golf. I can't get enough of the sport. There's only one thing about golf that I detest. That's the snooty attitude that prevails at some courses.

Take, for example, my recent experience at Crosswater Country Club in Sunriver, Oregon. It's ranked one of the best golf courses in the world. And they're not shy about reminding visitors of that fact.

While hacking there I noticed lateral hazards that were marked by both red and yellow stakes. Having never seen markings like that, my friend Doug asked the club pro for an explanation.

The pro's jaw dropped. Incredulously he sneered, "How long have you been playing golf?"

"About thirty years," Doug replied.

"And you don't know the difference between the red and yellow stakes?"

"Well, not when you have them marking the same lateral hazard."

"Well," the pro huffed, "what's your handicap?"

Doug told him and said, "Could you just answer my question?"

"A question that silly I'll have my understudy answer."

A kid whipped out a manual as thick as the Boston Yellow Pages and mumbled an explanation. I have forgotten his answer, but I will never forget that feeling of being shamed. I felt like Gomer Pyle at a banquet of five-star generals.

Unfortunately, that elitist attitude is not confined to country clubs. Sometimes it creeps into the church.

"I've been head elder for twenty-two years in this church, and nobody else is qualified to take over."

"Our church caters to the white-collar crowd."

"We can't trust the youth group to plan the worship service."

Our friend James leverages some blunt words against such bigots. His logic follows a natural progression of thought. First he states the thesis, next he illustrates it, then explains it, and finally he applies it.

First, find the thesis in James 2:1: "My brothers, as believers in our glorious Lord Jesus Christ, don't show favoritism." The thesis is simple: "Don't show favoritism."

Next, James illustrates:

> Suppose a man comes into your meeting wearing a gold ring and fine clothes, and a poor man in shabby clothes also comes in. If you show special attention to the man wearing fine clothes and say, "Here's a good seat for you," but say to the poor man, "You stand there" or "Sit on the floor by my feet," have you not discriminated among yourselves and become judges with evil thoughts? (James 2:1-4).

Perhaps a modern illustration would be helpful as well. In his excellent book, *The Measure of Our Days,* Dr. Jerome Groopman profiles eight of his patients.

One patient was Elizabeth. She scheduled the appointment herself, explaining that she had a blood disease and needed to see a specialist immediately. Assuming he would hear from her primary physician, Dr. Groopman agreed to the appointment. Much to Dr. Groopman's surprise, however, the woman sauntered into his office without any explanation of who sent her or how she got in.

Elizabeth was tall and big—a sixty-four-year-old woman sporting a thin smile, cool blue eyes, and puffed silver-gray hair. She dressed so as to disguise her ample figure; her double-strand pearl necklace and emerald earrings were subtle, yet worn to be noticed. At their initial encounter, Dr. Groopman disdained this lady.

"Dr. Groopman is quite an unusual name," she said before sharing any of her medical history. "Is it Dutch? Has your family been here long?"

"It is Dutch, and it is an unusual name," Dr. Groopman politely replied. "Actually, we're the only family I know of in the U.S. with that name. We're Jewish. My grandfather was originally from Kiev, in Russia. He escaped a pogrom in the 1880s and made his way to Amsterdam. The name Groopman was acquired there. He came to America in the early 1900s."

"What a charming story!" Elizabeth bubbled. "Well, we say in Boston that the mayor should be Irish, the barber Italian, and the doctor a Jew. We'll see, won't we?"

Dr. Groopman recoiled at her nerve. In his book he captures the tension of that moment:

> I sat speechless, uncertain how to respond. We had just met, she as a patient in need, I as the doctor she had sought out. Was her remark a benign attempt at upper-class humor or a provocation?

> If I ignored it, it might appear to be sign of weakness or shame about my identity. If I reacted sharply, it would divert us from the focus of the visit—her health—and I would not fulfill my role as a physician.[18]

That's when Dr. Groopman focused on a drawing that hung next to his desk. It pictured a man with a full black beard and white turban seated on a chair that rested on parallel pillars of Hebrew and English calligraphy. Directing Elizabeth's attention to that picture, he said, "That man is Moses Maimonides, a physician and rabbi who lived in the twelfth century. He worked in the court of the sultan of Cairo by day and cared for the destitute of that city by night. He began each day with the prayer that forms the two pillars:

> "Deem me worthy of seeing,
> In the sufferer
> Who seeks my advice,
> A person
> Neither rich nor poor,
> Friend nor foe,
> Good nor evil.
> Show me only the person." [19]

Dr. Groopman struggled to see only the person in Elizabeth. I, too, struggle to see only the person apart from social status or skin color. That's why I keep this ancient poem handy. I'm wondering: Could we not put a dent in the prejudice that poisons our world if we all lived this prayer? I'm surely willing to try. What about you?

To press our thinking in this area, James goes on to explain why the church should relentlessly shun favoritism. First, James says there is a theological reason. "Listen, my dear brothers: Has not God chosen those who are poor in the eyes of the world to be rich in faith and to inherit the kingdom he promised those who love him?"

(James 2:5). God's value system is upside down. The disenfranchised that are shunned on this earth will be elevated in the kingdom of God. Their value will be proportionate to their status as children of God, rather than being based on their material possessions.

According to James, God's love is universal and unconditional. God does not love us proportionate to our money or talent. God loves us unconditionally—in spite of what we are. And aren't you thankful?

This kind of love is often foreign to our way of behaving. The following poem captures the way we often love.

> Paul's girl is rich and haughty
> My girl is poor as clay
> Paul's girl is young and pretty
> My girl looks like a bale of hay
> Paul's girl is smart and clever
> My girl is dumb but good
> Ah, but would I trade my girl for Paul's?
> You bet your life I would!

That's how we often love, isn't it? Conditional love says I love you *if* . . .

if you loan me your car
if you laugh at my jokes and make me the center of attention
if you come home by curfew
if you will sleep with me
if you help me paint my house.
Conditional love says I love you *because* . . .
because you have gorgeous green eyes
because you have lots of money
because you are president of the company
because you hang around the right people
because you're a lot like me.

Genuine love says I love you *even though . . .*
even though you curse at me
even though you dye your hair purple and wear a dozen earrings
even though you don't share my belief in God
even though you smell bad
even though you have spread harmful rumors about me.

After giving a theological reason to love unconditionally—because that's how God's kingdom works—James offers a logical reason to shun favoritism. "But you have insulted the poor. Is it not the rich who are exploiting you? Are they not the ones who are dragging you into court? Are they not the ones who are slandering the noble name of him to whom you belong?" (James 2:6). James says, "Just think logically why it's crazy to show favoritism to the rich."

In that culture, it was legal for a creditor to choke a debtor and drag him to the bank and demand payment. The rich could legally exploit the poor. In fact, the only other place where that word "exploit" is used in the New Testament is to describe the tyrannical rule of Satan. And James asks, "Why do you butter up the very diabolical bullies who are abusing you? It is illogical."

Finally, James gives a biblical reason why it is wrong to show favoritism.

> If you really keep the royal law found in Scripture, "Love your neighbor as yourself," you are doing right. But if you show favoritism, you sin and you are convicted by the law as lawbreakers. For whoever keeps the whole law and yet stumbles at just one point is guilty of breaking all of it. For he who said, "Do not commit adultery" also said, "Do not murder." If you do not commit adultery but do commit murder, you have become a lawbreaker.

Favoritism is against the law of God. In sum, James is saying:

- Let Scripture be your standard.

- Let love be your law.
- Let mercy be your message.

Now it's time to apply the message. James counsels, "Speak and act as those who are going to be judged by the law that gives freedom, because judgment without mercy will be shown to anyone who has not been merciful. Mercy triumphs over judgment!" (James 2:12). Enough theory, he says. It's time to "speak and act" in a way that includes all people. No more favoritism, elitism, discrimination, bigotry, or chauvinism. Whatever label you use, it's prejudice plain and simple. And it has no business bleeding into the church.

I used to think that prejudice was something confined to history books. For example, I labeled it prejudice when the emperor of Rome ordered the mass execution of Christians. Prejudice sired the Gaelic feuds between Ireland and England and sent the Bolsheviks into a struggle with the Czarists. Prejudice caused the whimpering of Jewish children in the gas chambers of Auschwitz. In my mind, prejudice was always something that was "out there . . . in remote parts of the world . . . a long time ago."

Then Sharif transferred into our Christian academy. It was spring quarter, and students were looking for a distraction to get through the final few weeks of school. Sharif was the perfect distraction. He was from Iraq or Jordan or someplace like that, that you only hear about on the news. That didn't matter. What mattered was that he didn't fit in our culture. He dressed funny, smelled bad, and talked with an agitating accent.

A couple of the school jocks targeted "the foreign boy" for their entertainment. They wired his dorm room for a fireworks show at midnight and scorched the stuff in his half-empty closet. Another time, one of the cafeteria workers laced his chocolate-chip cookies with Ex-Lax—causing Sharif to miss an afternoon of classes. Then there was the time Sharif asked for help in preparing a speech for

English class. Some classmates peppered his script with some four-letter words.

When he delivered it, everyone roared with laughter. Everyone, that is, except Sharif. Suddenly Sharif stopped in the middle of his speech and looked up from the podium. Like a trapped tiger, his anxious eyes darted about the classroom of snickering students. Then he did something that surprised us all.

He cried.

Because Sharif came from a different culture, people treated him as if he really was different. You can call it prejudice. I call it sin. For prejudice is not a skin problem, it is a sin problem. When we saw Sharif's tears, finally our sin began to sink in. People nervously fidgeted and looked down while Sharif tried to regain his composure.

In class that day it hit us with fresh force that Sharif was not an animal, but a human being. He felt pain and hurt just like everyone else. While there were some things about Sharif that seemed different, his tears were no different than anyone else's.

I learned a lot in school. I learned about the Roman execution of Christians, the Gaelic feuds, and the horrors of the Holocaust. But more importantly, I learned that prejudice against people from other cultures is as rampant and wrong today as it ever has been. For this, we ought to be ashamed. For the same God who once proclaimed "There is neither Jew nor Greek, slave nor free, male nor female . . ." calls us to embrace *all* people. Until we learn that, we have no business calling ourselves Christians.

James 2:14-26

Extreme Faith

The story is told of a Mid-western town embroiled in a heat wave. The fields were thirsty, and the crops lay wilting. People anxiously searched the sky for any sign of relief. The arid days wore on like an unrelenting nightmare. No rain came.

The ministers of the local churches called for an hour of prayer on the town square the following Saturday. They asked everyone to bring an object of faith for inspiration.

On the appointed Saturday the townspeople crammed into the square. With fearful faces and hopeful hearts they prayed, clutching a variety of objects such as holy books, crosses, and rosaries. An hour later, as if on magical command, a drizzle began to blanket the crowd. People cheered as they waved their treasured objects high in thankfulness.

From the middle of the crowd one faith symbol towered above the rest: A nine-year-old child had brought an umbrella.

Living a faith-based life requires action. James asks: "What good is it, my brothers, if a man claims to have faith but has no deeds? Can such faith save him?" (James 2:14).

No doubt James would like the observation of T. C. Horton: "You can measure what you would do for the Lord by what you do." To hammer home the point, James offers three illustrations.

The first illustration is that of a person without clothes or food.

> Suppose a brother or sister is without clothes and daily food. If one of you says to him, "Go, I wish you well; keep warm and well fed," but does nothing about his physical needs, what good is it? In the same way, faith by itself, if it is not accompanied by action, is dead. But someone will say, "You have faith; I have deeds." Show me your faith without deeds, and I will show you my faith by what I do. You believe that there is one God. Good! Even the demons believe that—and shudder. You foolish man, do you want evidence that faith without deeds is useless? (James 2:15-20).

Faith without deeds has the value of a used Barry Manilow eight-track tape.

Want to test the authenticity of your faith? Look no further than what you do for those in need. You can exercise your faith by helping one person. Then look for another person in need. Don't wait until you see a naked child or a hungry prisoner, just start with the person closest to you.

Consider the words of Mother Teresa:

> I never look at the masses as my responsibility. I look at the individual. I can love only one person at a time. I can feed only one person at a time. Just one, one, one. You get closer to Christ by coming closer to each other. As Jesus said, "whatever you do to the least of my brethren, you do to me." So I begin … I begin. I picked up one person, maybe if I didn't pick up that one person, I wouldn't have picked up

the next 42,000. The whole work is only a drop in the ocean. But if I didn't put the drop in, the ocean would be one drop less. Same thing for you. Same thing in your family. Same thing in the church where you go, just begin ... one, one, one.[20]

Genuine faith manifests itself in action. You are God's answer for those who cry to Him for help. One poet captures it this way:

"On the street I saw a small girl
cold and shivering in a thin dress,
with little hope of a
decent meal.
I became angry and said to
God:
'Why did you permit this?
Why don't you do something
about it?'
For awhile God said nothing.
That night he replied, quite
suddenly:
'I certainly did something
about it.
I made you.' "[21]

Was not our ancestor Abraham considered righteous for what he did when he offered his son Isaac on the altar? You see that his faith and his actions were working together, and his faith was made complete by what he did. And the scripture was fulfilled that says, "Abraham believed God, and it was credited to him as righteousness," and he was called God's friend. You see that a person is justified by what he does and not by faith alone (James 2:21-24).

Remember the story? After a hundred years of begging, God finally grants Abraham his dream—a baby boy. What a raucous celebration that must have been—to welcome a child into the home of parents whose combined ages equaled 190! No wonder they named him *laughter*. John Ortberg describes the joy:

> Abraham and Sarah laughed at first because they didn't believe; they laughed at the sheer impossibility of it. They laughed because they were told they would have a son when they had reached an age when they didn't even dare to buy green bananas. And after the child was born, they laughed because they *did* believe. They laughed that when Sarah went to Wal-Mart, she was the only shopper to buy both Pampers and Depends. They laughed that both parents and baby had to eat the same strained vegetables because nobody in the whole family had a single tooth.[22]

"Then God said, 'Take your son, your only son, Isaac, whom you love, and go to the region of Moriah. Sacrifice him there as a burnt offering on one of the mountains I will tell you about' " (Genesis 22:2). Abraham isn't laughing anymore.

Nevertheless, he obeys. And by obeying, he becomes a poster child of faith. Faith, according to James, is about motion. It's about radical obedience to God. It's about doing—not just believing or understanding—but *doing* the will of God.

The illustration culminates in verse 24, where James makes a statement that was so radical it stirred Martin Luther to discredit the entire book. Luther wrote: "[James] does violence to Scripture, and so contradicts Paul and all Scripture. He tries to accomplish by emphasising law what the apostles bring about by attracting man to love. I therefore refuse him a place among the writers of the true canon of my Bible."[23]

Why all the hullabaloo about this verse? Well, for James to say "that a person is justified by what he does and not by faith alone" seems to fly in the face of the writings of Paul—not to mention Martin Luther's favorite sermon. To find harmony between the writings of James and Paul, one must grasp the unique context and emphasis of each author. Perhaps this chart can provide a helpful overview.

	Paul	**James**
Problem being addressed	Legalism	Laxity
"Works" **Focus**	Jewish laws Root of salvation (Internal/unseen)	Christian lifestyle Fruit of salvation (External/unseen)
Purpose	How to know that I'm a Christian	How to show that I'm a Christian

In sum, Paul tells us how to become a believer, while James tells us how to behave like a believer. Faith and deeds are not opposites. They are, in fact, inseparable. Actions validate one's faith. Works simply prove that it is faith. If there are no works it is not genuine faith, because by definition, works are a part of faith.

After dropping the theological bombshell in verse 24, James provides yet another illustration. "In the same way, was not even Rahab the prostitute considered righteous for what she did when she gave lodging to the spies and sent them off in a different direction? As the body without the spirit is dead, so faith without deeds is dead" (James 2:25-26).

Rahab was the prostitute who not only believed, but also acted on her belief. She hid two spies from Israel and saved their lives.

James could not have contrasted two people who were more opposite. Abraham was a man, Rahab was a woman. Abraham was a Jew, Rahab was a Gentile. Abraham was a patriarch, Rahab was a prostitute. Abraham was a somebody, Rahab was a nobody. The only thing the two had in common was their faith. Both had genuine faith that prompted them to act.

So what does that kind of vibrant faith look like today? Here are three more illustrations.

Pastor John Ortberg tells a delightful story about a high-school kid, Toby, who wrote an essay on world hunger and won a two-and-a-half-week mission trip to Ethiopia with World Vision. After working one morning at a distribution center, Toby tried to board the bus to go on the next assignment but was constrained by a local boy clamoring for his shirt. "Could I have your shirt?" he asked. The boy stood like an X-ray. He obviously had never owned a shirt like Toby's.

Because Toby felt that it would be too awkward working the rest of the day with no shirt, he blew off the beggar and boarded the bus. Toby gazed out the back window, trying not to focus on the half-naked locals chasing in their wake of dust. Toby would not see those kids again; but he would see them over and over in the video tattooed on his brain. He flipped open his Bible for comfort but landed instead on the searing words of Jesus in Matthew 25—"Whatever you do for the least of these . . . I needed clothing and you clothed Me."

After the mission trip, Toby returned home to Michigan, but he couldn't erase that kid from his mind. Every time he opened the Word it seemed evident that he had missed his calling to do the very thing that God most wanted him to do. At 1:00 A.M. one night Toby surrendered his sleep and retreated to his journal. Here are a few excerpts from his entry:

> "August 5, 1995
>
> "To all the children whose lives I crossed in Africa, I'm sorry. To every kid that I looked at and said 'yellum' which means 'I don't have,' I'm sorry. To every child that I passed by and gave nothing more than a smile, I'm sorry. To the boy who had only one shirt, if one could even call what he wore over his thin body a shirt, I'm so sorry. Please forgive me for keeping my shirt, for not ripping the shirt from my body and giving it to you—right then and right there; forgive me God for not obeying Your commands and giving to him who asks.

I'm sorry kid, you who had not eaten in two days. I'm sorry for bringing three suitcases of clothing with me and leaving with three plus some. Forgive me each of you; every time I feel sorry for myself, forgive my discontentment for every unfinished plate of food. Forgive the culture that I'm a part of, for my lack of care for others, for the unquenchable greediness for more things . . .

"Forgive me for forgetting you so quickly. May your faces be burned into my memory. I pray that I will never forget your thin faces or your worn clothes. . . . I pray that I will never forget your outstretched hands seeking to find my own—willing to accept them and me even though you knew that I had the world and was giving none of it to you, may I remember each of you as long as I live. Forgive me, all the things I take for granted—a free education, clean water, a toothbrush, a hot shower, a bowl of cereal any time of the day.

"God have mercy on me. Help me to use my blessings to fill the lives of those around me with happiness and joy. And God, most importantly to fill them with You."

The more Toby thought about it, the more he resolved to do something. So he launched a neighborhood campaign called "Give the Shirt off Your Back." Going door to door, he asked his neighbors, "Got an extra T-shirt?"

News of Toby's project spread. Television stations heralded the story and 7-Eleven stores positioned bins to collect T-shirts. Soon, Toby had 18,000 T-shirts.

After dumping the ones that had holes and stains (you know, the kind that your wife gets rid of when you're not looking—that favorite shirt that you've treasured ever since you made the basketball team at Shenandoah Valley Academy in 1980 but now it's gone because she put her own petty desires above your cherished memories—but I'm not bitter), Toby had 10,000 shirts ready to be shipped to Africa.

The next obstacle for Toby: How would he get them to Africa? He discovered that sending two tons of T-shirts via United Parcel Service would cost $65,000. So he called every relief organization he could find. The response was predictable, "Sorry, we can't help you."

After three months, officials from the warehouse storing the T-shirts gave Toby an ultimatum: "We've rented out the space so the shirts need to be gone in a week." So Toby prayed, "God, You got all these T-shirts together, now how are You going to get them to Africa?"

That's when Toby got a phone call from CNN, the news network. "Is this Toby, the T-shirt kid?"

"Yeah."

"We found a relief agency that can get your T-shirts over to Africa. They don't know what country, but they can get them to Africa."

A week later CNN followed up with a report. "We got your T-shirts to Africa. We dropped them off in a country where normally they'd never let something like that through customs, but we ended up using an Air Force jet and since the Air Force doesn't have to go through customs, they all made it—all 10,000. Now we hope it's OK, but the country where they ended up is Ethiopia."[24]

That's what faith looks like in our world today.

Dale Recinella wanted to put his faith into action. As one of the lawyers who negotiated the contracts for Dolphin Stadium and the Port of Miami, Dale enjoyed an income in the high six figures in the 1980s.

But Dale wanted more from life than big deals and big bucks. He wanted authentic faith. So he volunteered at the Good News Soup Kitchen in Tallahassee. Every day he'd arrive in his three-piece suit to help for about an hour and a half. He would stand by the door and chat with street people waiting to eat. This is what he writes:

> Before I came to Good News, "street people" was a meaningless term. It defined a group without defining anybody in particular. From the comfort of my car, my suburban home,

and my downtown law office, street people were just "those people out there somewhere."

Then one day an elderly woman named Helen came running to the Good News door. A man was chasing her and threatening to kill her if she didn't give him back his dollar. "Tell him he can't hit me 'cuz it's church property!" she pleaded. In true lawyerly fashion, I explained to her that Good News is not a church but he still couldn't hit her. After twenty minutes of failed mediation, I bought peace by giving each of them a dollar.

That evening, I happened to be standing on the corner of Park and Monroe. In the red twilight, I spied a lonely silhouette struggling in my direction from Tennessee Street. "Poor street person," I thought, as the figure inched closer. I was about to turn back to my own concerns when I detected something familiar in that shadowy figure. The red scarf. The clear plastic bag with white border. The unmatched shoes. "My God," I said in my thoughts, "that's Helen."

My eyes froze as she limped by and turned up Park. No doubt she would crawl under a bush to spend the night. My mind had always dismissed the sight of a street person in seconds. It could not expel the picture of Helen. That night, as I lay on my fifteen-hundred-dollar deluxe temperature-controlled waterbed, I couldn't sleep. A voice in my soul kept asking, "Where's Helen sleeping tonight?" No street person had ever interfered with my sleep, but the shadowy figure with the red scarf and the plastic bag had followed me home. I had made a fatal mistake. I had learned her name.

That's what faith looks like in our world today.

I have one more snapshot of faith—Sally. She was assigned the unlucky seat in front of me on a flight from Seattle to Houston. I say "unlucky" because I was traveling alone with my eleven-month-old daughter, Claire.

I'm not sure if Claire had colic, or she was tired, or she was growing a new tooth, or she just hates Continental Airlines. At any rate, she was fussier than a puppy in a flea bath.

It didn't help that we sat next to Mr. Businessman who thought his thigh had as much right to our seat as we did. He sneered and grunted as I squirmed to calm my kid. Finally I retreated to the aisle to rock Claire. After logging a chunk of very noisy frequent-flier miles, I returned to my seat in despair.

That's when I met Sally. She turned from her seat and said, "Would you like me to hold her for a while? I have more room with this empty seat next to me. Do you think she would come to me?"

"Absolutely." I flashed Claire one of those If-you-ever-want-to-see-your-binky-again looks and forked her over.

Suddenly . . . silence! "Whew," I gasped, "just in time to keep me from losing my last hair."

"What do you do?" she asked.

"I'm a pastor, and I could feel some nonpastoral words coming on!"

She laughed and turned to Claire. I escaped into the movie *What Women Want* and secretly fantasized that Sally might keep my kid for a while—not forever, just long enough for her to graduate from medical school. As it turned out, she entertained Claire until touch-down—much to the delight of everyone in the plane.

"Thank you," I said as we exited. "You're an angel."

"Now my husband would say that's not true," she said, blushing, "but since you're a pastor I can tell you that my goal every day is to show God's love in a tangible way. I'm glad I could help."

Had she never mentioned God I would have still labeled her a woman of faith. That's because faith is love in action. In fact, any "faith" that does not act in love will never fly in the real Word.

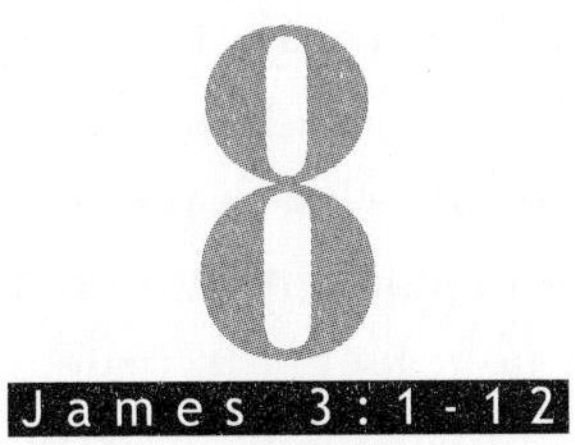

James 3:1-12

How to Lick Your Tongue

A student was sitting in church when the speaker stood to preach. Seeing who was preaching he remarked to the elderly woman next to him, "Oh, no! I can't believe he is preaching. That's my seminary teacher. We call him 'Old Stink.' I've already heard him five times this week. Had I known he was preaching, I would have stayed in bed."

"Um, ah," the woman stammered, "um, do you know who I am?"

"No."

"Well, then, allow me to introduce myself. I'm *Mrs.* Stink."

The student replied, "Do you know who I am?"

"No."

"Praise the Lord!" the student said.

Oh, be careful, little tongue, what you say. Once again, James admonishes us to guard the tongue. We have already studied his counsel to "be slow to speak." Then we considered the counsel to "keep a rein on your tongue. Fail to do this," James says, "and your religion is worthless."

Once again, James tackles the topic with the subtlety of a nuclear bomb. "Be careful, little tongue, what you say," James tells us, "because the tongue harnesses incredible power."

Ironic, isn't it? After all, what is the tongue, really? It's a four-inch, two-ounce slab of mucous membrane that houses an array of nerves and muscles to help us chew, taste, and talk. That's it. Yet James argues that it's an instrument of extraordinary power.

Recently I had a front-row seat to a demonstration of breathtaking power—the implosion of the Kingdome in Seattle, Washington. While it was yet dark we arrived on the 12th Street Bridge to claim prime real estate with an unobstructed view.

Anticipation mounted. Thousands assembled to share this moment of history.

While we waited, TV reporter Lori Matsakowa happened by. "Would you like to be a contestant for a game like 'Who Wants to Be a Millionaire?' " she asked.

"Sure," I said.

"We'll go live in about twenty minutes, and you'll play against other opponents until you either get eliminated or win."

"OK!"

As fate would have it, I won—even though I missed the final question by a modest eighty million! Don't laugh unless you know how many cubic inches of air there are in the Kingdome. I guessed closer than my opponent did, so I won the grand prize—a mug. (Don't ask me why they called it "Who Wants to Be a *Millionaire?*")

The festivities, of course, were just filler leading up to the big bang. At 8:30 A.M. all eyes were glued to the Kingdome. After waiting three hours, we heard a thundering explosion and in a matter of seconds the Seattle landmark was reduced to rubble.

Talk about power. How a relatively small amount of dynamite can do such breathtaking damage is beyond me.

James makes a similar point. He says that our words have dynamite-like power. Of course the metaphors available to him in the first century were things such as horses and ships and forest fires.

Nevertheless, he uses the imagery to illustrate the power of the tongue.

James observes how you can take a small piece of metal—a bit in the mouth of a horse—and control the actions of a thousand-pound animal. He notes that a small appendage on the stern of a ship can affect the direction of an ocean-going vessel. Then he notes how a single spark can start a raging forest fire.

If James were preaching today, he might point out how a few sticks of dynamite can level 130,000 tons of concrete. Yet, if you put the power of the Kingdome implosion against the tongue, James would argue that it is no contest. The tongue wins hands down. Proportionate to the size of our bodies the tongue is very small, but the power it possesses is staggeringly large.

Why is the tongue so powerful? James offers three reasons. First he notes that the tongue has the power to direct our lives.

> When we put bits into the mouths of horses to make them obey us, we can turn the whole animal. Or take ships as an example. Although they are so large and are driven by strong winds, they are steered by a very small rudder wherever the pilot wants to go. Likewise the tongue is a small part of the body, but it makes great boasts (James 3:3-5).

In a similar fashion to how a bit controls the direction of a horse, or the rudder controls the direction of a ship, so the tongue controls the direction of a life. In fact, words can control the destiny of entire corporations. Take, for example, the slump in sales that McDonald's restaurants sustained when the rumor got out that Ronald McDonald and his Golden Arch cohorts were using earthworms as protein substitute in their burgers. The rumor spread like . . . well, like worms after an April rain. During that time, had you mentioned the topic of earthworms around the headquarters in Oak Brook, Illinois, you would likely have been bombed with a dozen sesame-seed buns.

The king of greasy eats had to launch an aggressive campaign to polish up its reputation. Such is the power of words.

It has been estimated that most people speak enough words in one week to fill a large 500-page book. In the average lifetime this would amount to 3,000 volumes or 1,500,000 pages! It is sobering to think that by these words we will either be "acquitted" or "condemned" on the day of judgment. " 'But I tell you,' " Jesus warned, " 'that men will have to give account on the day of judgment for every careless word they have spoken. For by your words you will be acquitted, and by your words you will be condemned.' " (Matthew 12:36, 37). In other words, words direct one's eternal destiny.

So what kind of life are you shaping with your words? Only you can build the legacy you want to leave. And remember that your building blocks are the words you use. So grab the steering wheel of your life today and take control of your destiny by using uplifting and life-enriching words. Here are some words for practice:

"Congratulations."

"I love you."

"There are seconds on dessert."

"You look great."

"You are right."

"I'm sorry."

"My treat."

"Can I help you with that?"

"I prayed for you last night."

They are simple words that pack a profound punch. Give them a try.

Of course, words not only direct our lives in noble ways; they can destroy as well. Again, consider some examples.

"You're a loser."

"Divorce is granted."

"I hate you."

"The tumor is malignant."

"I don't care what you think."

"No."

"Get a real job."

"You're on your own."

"Can't you do anything right?"

James alludes to the destructive power of words:

> Consider what a great forest is set on fire by a small spark. The tongue also is a fire, a world of evil among the parts of the body. It corrupts the whole person, sets the whole course of his life on fire, and is itself set on fire by hell. All kinds of animals, birds, reptiles and creatures of the sea are being tamed and have been tamed by man, but no man can tame the tongue. It is a restless evil, full of deadly poison (James 3:5-8).

The tongue can reek the same havoc as a forest fire. It can destroy people. James says the tongue can corrupt the whole person and set the whole course of his life on fire and it is itself set on fire by hell.

It's interesting to note that the Greek word translated "hell" is not *hades,* but rather *geena* (gheh'-en-nah)—the name for the Valley of Hinnom just outside the walls of Jerusalem. Scripture describes *geena* as a place of unquenchable fire where maggots worked to destroy the carcasses tossed into it. What a graphic word picture of the destructive power of the tongue!

As a fire, the tongue is "a world of evil," James declares. The word "evil" is *adikia.* Again, it is a very strong word denoting moral unrighteousness. It is the same word used by Paul when he states, " 'Everyone who confesses the name of the Lord must turn away from wickedness' " (2 Timothy 2:19).

The inflammatory language that James uses pictures the tongue as a power that carries enormous potential for destruction. We've all seen that power, haven't we?

I read once of a woman's suicide note that simply read, "They said . . ." She didn't complete the sentence, but something "they said" killed her. That's the deadly power that James is talking about.

Next, James likens the tongue to "all kinds of animals" that cannot be tamed. The Greek word that is translated "restless" literally means "always likely to snap or to breakout." Such is the case even with animals that have been tamed.

Several years ago I attended the taping of a local TV show in Seattle. The invited guest that day was not a celebrity or a sports star or a politician. Rather, the guest of honor was a tiger.

The top local news story at the time was of an animal trainer in my hometown of Bothell who had a tiger escape his training compound. Tragically, the beast killed an innocent man before it was captured again. The show featured the trainer defending his animal. To prove that his tiger was perfectly safe, he announced that he was going to bring the animal onstage at the end of the show, constrained by only a leash.

The moment he announced his intentions, a spirit of uneasiness swallowed the crowd. Rigor mortis seized my body—which incidentally, was plopped on the front row. Why? Because with wild animals you never know what might happen. You can't really tame a tiger. A tiger is a tiger is a tiger. I have never felt so relieved to leave a TV studio alive!

Similarly, James says our tongues cannot be tamed; there is always that same threat to snap. Like an animal or a fire, the tongue can destroy.

I was reminded of this recently when I spoke for the homecoming weekend at my first parish. Following an afternoon dedication ceremony, one of the charter members approached me. "Um, excuse me, Pastor, but could I talk to you before you leave?"

"Sure."

We escaped to a private office, and he spilled his story.

"I don't know if you remember the organizational meeting on April 24, 1991, but I need to unpack some things about that meeting. Ten years later, I still feel wounded by your words."

I remembered the meeting because some candid and harsh words were exchanged. Although the meeting was ten years behind us, he could recall my every word.

"Because of what you said, I stopped attending church. For a decade now, I have felt so angry and bitter toward you. I even entertained thoughts of physically harming you."

Then his expression softened. "But through all of this, God has gently been prompting me to let it go and return to church. While I resisted for years, I decided that after you moved to another parish I'd come back to this church. Thanks for listening. I felt this conversation was important for me to feel closure on the issue."

"Um, well, I don't know what to say," I stammered, "except that I, ah, well, am sorry. Your story feels like a sledgehammer to my heart."

We prayed and hugged and went our different ways, but not before a reminder that words can destroy.

Conversely, words can edify. I file those words. Whenever I feel a few curves short of a smiley face I pull out my collection of torn notes and faded letters. Some date back to the days when I had hair on my head and none on my legs. (That's a long time ago!) The file isn't much, but it's a Power Bar to a bruised spirit. Take a peek:

From a kid in my congregation after they sang "Happy Birthday" to me to celebrate my fortieth.

"Dear Pastor Karl,
Ura good pastor. I like your funny stories.
Your friend,
Ryan
P. S. You don't look a day older than 39."

From the students at Shenandoah Valley Academy:

"Dear Karl,
Your presence here on this campus has been a true blessing for

all of us. Your brilliant and witty stories have uplifted us and made us realize that Christianity can be fun. You have also helped us understand that God's love is unconditional and ever-accepting."

Solomon said it well: "The tongue of the righteous is choice silver, but the heart of the wicked is of little value" (Proverbs 10:20). Indeed, words wisely spoken are like fine silver. On the other hand, wicked words have little value—they flow out of an evil heart. Hence, the statement that James makes next. Note how the tongue discloses what is in the heart.

> With the tongue we praise our Lord and Father, and with it we curse men, who have been made in God's likeness. Out of the same mouth come praise and cursing. My brothers, this should not be. Can both fresh water and salt water flow from the same spring? My brothers, can a fig tree bear olives, or a grapevine bear figs? Neither can a salt spring produce fresh water (James 3:9-12).

Justin the Martyr once said, "By examining the tongue of the patient, physicians find out the diseases of the body, and philosophers the diseases of the mind." Our words disclose who we really are.

Sociologists claim that we judge intelligence based on vocabulary. I judge your smarts by the words you use, and you do the same to me.

I picked up on this at an early age. When I was a kid my dad would recite to his three sons a wordy explanation that scientists used to explain why the animals went into Noah's ark. Because it was packed with big words that made us feel intelligent all three of us boys memorized it.

After a cross-country move, the first Sabbath in a new church my brothers and I were sitting in Sabbath School. This tiny church had just one children's division to accommodate all ages. Naturally the teacher was delighted to have three new kids in her small class.

As it happened, the lesson that week was on Noah. One of the first questions she asked was "Why did the animals go into the ark?" Immediately my brothers and I threw up our hands. The teacher pointed our direction. Without missing a beat we recited in three-part harmony: "It was due to the innate compulsion of the animal kingdom, superimposed by the posterior sphere of the cerebral afterglow, sensitizing ever centility of the corporillity of the brute creation. Thus affecting a translocation of materialistic concept which leads to a more salubrious environment."

The teacher immediately jumped to a conclusion regarding our intelligence. While her assessment was not accurate, we fooled her just because of our words.

Our words not only disclose our mental aptitude, but our spiritual condition as well. The tongue displays who we are. James asks, "Can fresh water and salt water come from the same spring?" Ludicrous. How about a fig tree? Can it bear olives? Or a grapevine bear figs? Of course not! If you plant a peach tree, you don't get watermelons (unless I plant it, in which case you get weeds).

James is saying the real issue is the heart. The tongue simply displays what is in the heart. Show me someone with a harsh tongue, and I'll show you an angry heart. Show me someone with a boasting tongue, and I'll show you an insecure heart. Show me someone with a gossiping tongue, and I'll show you an unconverted heart.

On the other hand, show me someone who speaks kindness, and I will show you a tender heart. Show me someone who speaks in humility, and I will show you a secure heart. Show me someone who speaks words of encouragement, and I can tell you what is in her heart. Jesus said it well: " 'For out of the overflow of the heart the mouth speaks' " (Matthew 12:34).

The following parable from my book *I'd Rather Kiss a Catfish* illustrates this.

I felt like a rag doll in the dryer's spin cycle. Desperate to feel better, I made an appointment with Dr. Law.

"It's your heart," Dr. Law growled with the compassion of a bulldog.

"My heart?" I questioned. "There's no trace of heart trouble in my family. At least examine me."

"No diagnosis necessary" he snapped, "it's your heart."

"My heart has never given me problems. But my feet—oh boy, there's the problem! These feet have taken me to liquor stores and nightclubs and—"

"It's your heart."

"Doctor, please check out my hands. These lousy, dysfunctional hands have rolled dice, played cards, filled mugs with beer. Here's the problem," I insisted.

"It's not your hands, it's your heart."

"At least examine my ears. These ears have listened to dirty jokes and gossip and profanity and enough rock 'n' roll to kill the Rolling Stones."

"It's your heart."

"There's plenty of other doctors in this city!" I stormed out of his office like a stuntman from a cannon.

For the next ten months, I bounced from doctor to doctor to doctor—faithfully performing every prescription, yet never feeling healthy. Dr. Religion prescribed a regimen of baptism, church attendance, and tithing. Dr. Diet blamed my eating habits and suggested a menu of tofu, tree bark, and Garden Burgers. Dr. B. Good stripped off my rings and bracelet and helped me stop going to movies.

While every doctor promised a cure, nothing could quiet the gnawing emptiness that ached within. In despair, I returned to Dr. Law.

"It's your heart," were Dr. Law's first words.

"Yeah, yeah," I barked. "So what do I do?"

"You need a heart transplant."

"Glad it's nothing serious." My cynicism leaked like poison.

"Heart transplant or death." His words cut like a scalpel.

"OK, I'll let you do the operation."

"Oh, I don't operate," said Dr. Law, "that's what I have a partner for. Follow me."

He led me across the hall to Dr. Grace's office.

"Are you ready for the operation?" Dr. Grace asked kindly.

"I, um, ah, I, ah . . ."

"Relax, I have never lost a case."

"OK, but give me a double dose of anesthetic."

"Oh no," he said with a chuckle. "I want you awake for this so you can tell others about it."

Even my toenails were sweating as he made the first incision. Suddenly the odor of pure manure filled the room.

"Peeeeeeee-yeeeeeeeeew," I shouted, grabbing a pillow to breathe through. "What is that disgusting smell?"

"It's your heart."

"My heart?"

"You can smell the dirty jokes and the gossip and the pornography—they've all collected here in your heart."

"I guess I really do need a new heart. By the way, what does a heart cost these days? I haven't seen any heart sales lately."

"Twenty-six million dollars," he said without looking up.

"Twenty-six million dol—um, ah, at fifty bucks a month, how long will this take to pay for?"

"You'll never pay for it," he said, chuckling again. "A Friend has taken care of it for you." Making his final stitch, Dr. Grace looked up. "There, how does that feel?"

"I feel better already," I said.

"You'll feel even better with exercise."

"Exercise?"

"Dr. Law and I are firm believers in exercise."

"Like the other doctors prescribed?"

"In a sense," Dr. Grace said. "Exercise is critical, but only after you have addressed the heart of the matter—which is a matter of the heart."

My mind swirled like a tornado. "About the Friend who paid for my new heart—um, could I, ah, meet Him?"

"Most certainly," Dr. Grace said, smiling. "Oh, ah, but be prepared. In order to give you a new heart, His was crushed. So don't be surprised by the ugly, gaping scar in His side."

Wondering about the condition of your heart? Listen to yourself speak.

The tongue has inconceivable power—the power to direct, the power to destroy, and the power to disclose the condition of the heart. So how do we harness this power and lick the temptation of the tongue?

When it comes to licking the tongue, sheer willpower is not enough. David expresses this reality in Psalm 39 when he records his resolution:

> "I will watch my ways and keep my tongue from sin; I will put a muzzle on my mouth as long as the wicked are in my presence." But when I was silent and still, not even saying anything good, my anguish increased. My heart grew hot within me, and as I meditated, the fire burned; then I spoke with my tongue (Psalm 39:1-3).

David discovered the futility of trying to lick the tongue by sheer willpower. We could wear muzzles and still falter when it comes to controlling our words. That's because words flow out of what is in the heart. To control our words we must have converted hearts.

Thus my daily prayer is this poem:

> Let the words of my mouth
> and the meditation of my heart
> be acceptable in Thy sight, O God.
> If it were only a matter of words,
> I'd have no problem.
> But it's not
> And I do.
> So God, please . . .
> mold the meditation of my heart.

It's not just the words that trip us up; it's the meditation of the heart. Unless the meditation of the heart is continually focused on Jesus, the tongue will not be tamed. Jesus said as much in John 15:7. " 'If you remain in me and my words remain in you, ask whatever you wish, and it will be given you.' " There's the key to taming the tongue. As you remain in Jesus, His words will remain in you. That's a promise from Jesus Himself. If you want to lick the tongue, you must live in Christ.

Charles Trumbull wrote, " 'Jesus Christ does not want to be our helper; He wants to be our life. He does not want us to work for Him. He wants us to let Him do His work through us. When our life is not only Christ's but Christ, our life will be a winning life; for He cannot fail.' "[25]

Don't skim that final line. It's the key to controlling your conversations. Yes, there is power in the tongue. But there is greater power still in Christ. Indeed, you can experience a winning life, for Jesus cannot fail.

9

James 3:13-18

Time to Wise Up

Gary, a young businessman from Detroit, Michigan, craved some quiet. So he hopped a plane to Key West, Florida. For two weeks he ambled down the beaches collecting shells, uniquely patterned rocks, and unusually shaped driftwood.

On one of his beach-combing forays, he eyed a conspicuous hole puncturing a sandstone cliff. He scaled the precipice and peered into the hole.

Thinking he might have discovered an abandoned bird's nest, he stuck his hand deep inside. He groped around until his hand rested on what felt like peanut M&M's.

Hoping they were bird's eggs, he retrieved twenty-three of them. But when he looked at them closely, he saw only hard, gray, clay balls varying in size from a large pea to a golf ball.

Disappointed, Gary dumped the clay balls into his pocket and resumed strolling along the beach. That evening he used the clay balls like BB's, flinging them into the ocean at targets of floating driftwood. By the time he reached his hotel, all the clay balls were gone—or so he thought.

After the two-week vacation, Gary returned home to Detroit. While doing his laundry, he found one more clay ball in the pocket of his bathing suit. Reminiscing the good times at the beach, he tossed it into a dish of vitamin tablets, stray buttons, and spare change.

Months later, Gary met Bert at work, and they became friends. Bert's passion was reading tales of pirate ships and buried treasures in Key West. Gary could visualize the whole scene that Bert described: peg legs, eye patches, sea captains, and treasure chests of gold and diamonds buried in the beaches of southern Florida.

One morning at work Bert told Gary how pirates would hide precious jewels from their enemies by molding wet clay around gems and then hiding the clay balls in holes on the sandstone cliffs.

Surely, Gary thought, *that's not what I found.*

Gary's curiosity was piqued enough to justify skipping work that afternoon. He went home to reexamine the remaining clay ball.

Pawing through the junk dish, he uncovered it. With a knife he scraped away at the clay. At first there was nothing but clay. Then the ball cracked. Out rolled a small but perfect blue-white diamond.

Gary felt paralyzed by his discovery. Then he remembered the handful of clay marbles that he had buried in the ocean's tides.

For me, the story rings too familiar. Often I've played the fool of Gary. I have mishandled treasures hidden in God's Word that reveal how to live in the best possible way. Ignoring the wisdom of the Word is like trashing treasures that could truly make us rich.

The wisest man in history put it this way:

> Happy is the person who finds wisdom, the one who gets understanding. Wisdom is worth more than silver; it brings more profit than gold. Wisdom is more precious than rubies; nothing you could want is equal to it. With her right hand wisdom offers you a long life, and with her left hand she gives you riches and honor. Wisdom will make your life pleasant and will bring you peace (Proverbs 3:13-17, NCV).

Sounds inviting, doesn't it? Imagine a life that is "pleasant" and characterized by "peace." Such is the life of wisdom. James calls us to this kind of life. "Who is wise and understanding among you? Let him show it by his good life, by deeds done in the humility that comes from wisdom" (James 3:13). As we have come to expect, James challenges us to live a life of wisdom rather than to simply talk about it. "Show me your wisdom" James says. "Don't tell me about it. Talk is cheap, remember?"

What is wisdom? Bill Hybels defines it like this: "Wisdom is what is true and right combined with good judgment. Other words that fit under the umbrella of the biblical concept of wisdom are *discerning, judicious, prudent* and *sensible.* Not very glamorous words, perhaps, but words you can build a life on."[26]

That's what James is interested in—words to build a life on. Sitting in the classroom is not enough. You may get an education that way, but you may miss a life of wisdom. While I believe in formal education (I work on a university campus where education is esteemed right up there with life, liberty, and the pursuit of a quicker-setting Jell-O), I see the limits of education apart from wisdom. For example, I have plenty of degrees, but I can't even change the oil in my car. My brothers call me "The most educated person alive with no useful skills." What good can heaps of education do if it doesn't help us in real life?

I suspect G. K. Chesterton was right when he said, "Without education, we are in a horrible and deadly danger of taking educated people seriously." Sadly, I know too many brains who have a B.S., an M.A., a Ph.D. but no L.I.F.E.

Truth is, my best teachers have been folk who don't necessarily park lots of initials after their names. They're ordinary wayfarers with extraordinary wisdom.

Their class is called Life 101. Their classroom is the real world. And their textbook is a compilation of one-liners that they've learned along the way. Listen to their wisdom, as recorded in Ken Davis's book, *Lighten up!*

"I've learned you can't hide a piece of broccoli in a glass of milk" (age 7).

"I've learned that when I wave to people in the country, they stop what they're doing and wave back" (age 9).

"I've learned that if I want to cheer myself up, I should try cheering someone else up" (age 13).

"I've learned that although it's hard to admit it, I'm secretly glad my parents are strict with me" (age 15).

"I've learned that wherever I go, the world's worst drivers have followed me there" (age 29).

"I've learned that the greater a person's sense of guilt, the greater his need to cast blame on others" (age 46).

"I've learned that children and grandparents are natural allies" (age 46).

"I've learned that singing 'Amazing Grace' can lift my spirits for hours" (age 49).

"I've learned that motel mattresses are better on the side away from the phone" (age 50).

"I've learned that you can tell a lot about a man by the way he handles these three things: a rainy day, lost luggage, and tangled Christmas tree lights" (age 52).

"I've learned that regardless of your relationship with your parents, you miss them terribly after they die" (age 53).

"I've learned that making a living is not the same thing as making a life" (age 58).

"I've learned you shouldn't go through life with a catcher's mitt on both hands. You need to be able to throw something back" (age 64).

"I've learned that if you pursue happiness, it will elude you. But if you focus on your family, the needs of others, your work, meeting new people, and doing the very best you can—happiness will find you" (age 65).

"I've learned that everyone can use a prayer" (age 72).

"I've learned that even when I have pains, I don't have to be one" (age 82).

"I've learned that every day you should reach out and touch someone. People love that human touch: holding hands, a warm hug, or just a friendly pat on the back" (age 85).

"I've learned that I still have a lot to learn" (age 90).

Some choice wisdom there, don't you think? Wisdom informs us of the best way to do life. In his discussion on wisdom, James makes a distinction between worldly wisdom and heavenly wisdom.

First, James speaks of worldly wisdom.

> But if you harbor bitter envy and selfish ambition in your hearts, do not boast about it or deny the truth. Such "wisdom" does not come down from heaven but is earthly, of the devil. For where you have envy and selfish ambition, there you find disorder and every evil practice (James 3:14-16).

According to the passage, there are two defining marks of worldly wisdom: envy and selfish ambition. The following parable helps us to see this.

Once upon a time there were three people who lived on the same cul-de-sac. Their names were Danny, Candy, and Rick. They lived in cozy homes in a quiet neighborhood with meticulously manicured lawns. They all thought highly of one another.

Then Danny thought he saw Candy peering enviously at his rose garden with its rare blooms, so he bought an air rifle and slept with it under his pillow. Rick heard about this, so he also bought an air rifle—just in case it was ever needed. Before long, Candy bought one too.

Danny figured he'd best stay one step ahead so he traded in his air rifle for a double-barreled shotgun, and he changed the locks on his home one morning after church. Candy and Rick heard about this and quickly did the same. Then Rick grumbled about how his neighbors could see into his yard, so he erected an eight-foot fence around his property with curled barbed wire at the top of it. Danny did the same—except his barbed wire was electrified. Candy not only installed electric barbed wire, but purchased an arsenal of hand grenades as well—just in case.

One night, when they figured no one was watching, Danny and Candy went to the weapon store to buy something a bit more powerful. Danny bought napalm while Candy was interested in the poisonous chemicals that could be sprayed in a gas. Rick, on the other hand, was busy in his basement perfecting something he called "nuclear."

Meanwhile their houses were deteriorating, they did not have enough money to buy clothes and food for their families, their gardens were overcome with weeds, it was too dangerous to let their kids ride bikes in the cul-de-sac, and there was no time left to enjoy life any more.[27]

Can you see where envy and selfish ambition leads? No wonder James teaches that worldly wisdom leads to "disorder and every evil practice."

In contrast, notice the marks of heavenly wisdom. "But the wisdom that comes from heaven is first of all pure; then peace-loving, considerate, submissive, full of mercy and good fruit, impartial and sincere. Peacemakers who sow in peace raise a harvest of righteousness" (James 3:17, 18).

James shares seven qualities in a person with genuine wisdom. You might think of them as habits of highly effective Christians. Let's look at each one.

1. Pure

First and foremost, heavenly wisdom is pure. Stephen Covey, author of the classic bestseller, *The Seven Habits of Highly Effective People,* starts his description of highly effective people in the same place as James did. "In the last analysis," says Covey, "what we *are* communicates far more eloquently than anything we *say* or *do*. We all know it. There are people we trust absolutely because we know their character. Whether they're eloquent or not, whether they have the human relations techniques or not, we trust them, and we work successfully with them."[28]

A story bouncing around the Internet tells of an emperor in the Far East who was growing old. He knew it was coming time to choose his successor. Instead of choosing one of his own children, however, he decided to do something different. He called all the young people in the kingdom and said, "It has come time for me to choose the next emperor. I have decided to choose one of you."

The kids were shocked! The emperor continued. "I am going to give each one of you a seed today. It is a very special seed. I want you to go home, plant the seed, water it, and come back here one year from today with what you have grown from this one seed. I will then judge the plants that you bring to me, and the one I choose will be the next emperor of the kingdom!"

A boy named Ling was there that day. Like the others, he received a seed. He went home and excitedly told his mother the whole story. She helped him get a pot and some planting soil. He planted the seed and watered it carefully. Every day he nurtured the seed. After about three weeks, some of the other youths talked about their seeds and the plants that were beginning to grow. Ling kept checking his seed, but nothing grew. Three weeks, four weeks, five weeks went by. Still nothing.

By now others were talking about their plants. Ling had no plant. He felt like a failure. Six months went by, and still nothing in Ling's pot. He just knew he had killed his seed. Everyone else had trees and tall plants, but he had nothing. Ling didn't say anything to his friends, however. He just kept waiting for his seed to grow.

A year went by and all the youths of the kingdom brought their plants to the emperor for inspection. Ling told his mother that he wasn't going to take an empty pot. But she encouraged him to go and to be honest about what happened. Ling felt sick to his stomach, but he knew his mother was right. He took his empty pot to the palace.

When Ling arrived, he was amazed at the variety of plants grown by all the other youths. They were beautiful, in all shapes and sizes.

Ling put his empty pot on the floor while many of the other kids laughed at him.

When the emperor arrived, he surveyed the room and greeted the young people. Ling just tried to hide in the back. "My, what great plants, trees, and flowers you have grown," said the emperor. "Today, one of you will be appointed the next emperor!"

All of a sudden, the emperor spotted Ling at the back of the room with his empty pot. He ordered his guards to bring him to the front. Ling was terrified. "The emperor knows I'm a failure! Maybe he will have me killed!"

When Ling got to the front, the emperor asked his name. "My name is Ling," he replied. All the kids were laughing and making fun of him. The emperor asked everyone to quiet down then announced to the crowd, "Behold your new emperor! His name is Ling!" Ling couldn't believe it. How could he be the new emperor?

Then the emperor said, "One year ago today, I gave everyone here a seed. I told you to take the seed, plant it, water it, and bring it back to me today. But I gave you all boiled seeds that would not grow. All of you, except Ling, have brought me trees and plants and flowers. When you found that the seed would not grow, you substituted another seed for the one I gave you. Ling was the only one with the courage and honesty to bring me a pot with my seed in it. Therefore, he is the one who will be the new emperor!"

In the end, purity of character pays. So pay close attention to character.

2. Peace-loving

It is the wise person that promotes peace. I know of a fellow who is so antagonistic he will only eat food that disagrees with him. Have you ever known somebody like that? A highly effective Christian will seek relational harmony.

Lloyd Ogilvie writes, "Peace is the result of grace. It literally means, 'To bind together.' In other words, the peace which comes from unmerited, unearned love can weave and bind our fragmented lives into wholeness. And the civil war of divergent drives, which makes us feel like rubber bands stretched in all directions, is ended. The Lord is in control. He has forgiven the past, He is in charge of now, and shows the way for each new day."[29]

3. Considerate

Next, James says that highly effective Christians are considerate. The Greek word describes someone who goes beyond the letter of the law to administer the most merciful judgment. A considerate person is someone who knows when it is wrong to apply the strict letter of the law. She knows how to forgive when strict justice gives her the right to condemn.

It is the same Greek word used to describe Jesus when He dealt with the prostitute who was caught in the act and the Pharisees wanted to stone her. Even though she legally should have been stoned, Jesus went beyond the letter of the law and was considerate of her.

Recently I was in a parking lot as a car and a pick-up rolled toward the same parking space. Both were obviously determined to seize the space. A grizzly mountain man rolled down his window in his one-ton pick-up. An Ivana Trump look-alike rolled down the window of her white Cadillac.

I rolled down my window. (It's sanctified eavesdropping since I knew it would make a juicy illustration for this book.)

The man hollered, "Back it off, Lady. I was here first."

"Tough luck, fellow. You're coming in from the wrong direction. You can't do that."

"%#&*@%^^!"

"The rule is, the car to the stall first gets to park there. I was here first, so beat it!"

"But my truck's bigger. So stick it with your rules."

The lady pulled forward an inch. The mountain man pulled forward an inch. The lady got an inch closer, the mountain man pulled closer. Their bumpers were literally touching. Both refused to budge.

Finally, I pulled away to park three spaces down from their feud. There were dozens of spaces. But they weren't interested in parking. Talk about wise and *other*wise! I'd file those hostile drivers in the latter category.

That's what James is saying. Wise people are considerate. They are flexible in their application of the strict letter of the law.

4. Submissive

The next characteristic of a highly effective Christian is submission. The Greek word here describes a person who is always approachable and open to reason. Have you ever known a spiritual know-it-all—someone who has it all figured out, and they don't care to hear any differing opinions?

It's that mentality of "We are the select few, let all the rest be damned. There's room enough in hell for you, we'll not have heaven crammed." James says that attitude is unwise. Highly effective Christians are always learning more.

5. Full of mercy and good fruit

Jesus told lots of stories to support this characteristic of highly effective Christians. Here's an updated parable to chew on:

On one occasion a hotshot attorney stood up to skewer Jesus. "Teacher," he sparred, "What do I have to do to get to heaven?"

The teacher answered, "Hmmmm, what do you think?"

"Well, I guess I need to love God and love my neighbor as much as I love myself." The lawyer couldn't swallow his smug smirk.

"Very good," Jesus said and smiled. "Go do it, and you'll be saved."

The lawyer blushed. To have asked a profound question only to get a simple answer, and then to have answered his own question; he was caught by surprise but not by silence. Quickly he ventured a comeback: "Ah, but *who* is my neighbor?"

In reply Jesus said: "A prostitute with AIDS was working the strip by Pike Place Market in Seattle, when she fell into the hands of hefty colleagues. They resented the disease she was smearing across their profession so they stripped her of her clothes, beat her, and went away, leaving her half dead.

"Some church folk happened by who couldn't be sidetracked on their beeline to prayer meeting. The only acknowledgment of the victim came from one plump lady, who whispered, 'We surely need to move our church to the suburbs soon. You know, away from all this lowlife.'

"So too, an off-duty policeman came to the place and saw her. *If I'm not getting paid then I'm not getting involved,* he thought.

"But a doctor, as he traveled, came where the woman was; and when he saw her, he took pity on her. He covered her with his coat and bandaged her wounds. Then he put the woman in his Lexus and drove her to Harbor View Medical Center.

"Flipping his Platinum Visa to the receptionist he said, 'Put her in the best room you have. I don't want her on the AIDS ward because I've seen patients there who are raped of their dignity. This woman deserves the best so give it to her at any cost. When I return, I will reimburse you for any extra expense you may have.'

" 'Whatever you say,' the receptionist said and nodded.

"No sooner did the doctor disappear than the hallway was buzzing with gossip. 'Wasn't that the guy on TV?' queried a nurse. 'I think he was,' answered another. 'Surely not,' offered a third. 'He would never—wait a minute, look at the name on the credit card.' The women gasped in disbelief.

Then Jesus asked, "So who was the neighbor to the prostitute?"

The expert in the law replied, "Well, I, um, guess it was that doctor guy."

"Bingo," Jesus said, glaring like Clint Eastwood. "Now go and do like Dr. Kavorkian did on that night."

Let us be careful not to judge others. Faith is full of mercy and good fruit. The one who has these qualities will qualify as a wise neighbor.

6. Impartial

The Greek word here means "unwavering." A highly effective Christian is a person who is committed—no matter the cost.

Frankly, there are too many weathervane Christians. They point whichever way the wind is blowing. It seems to me that much of our religious activity today is nothing more than a cheap anesthetic we use to deaden the pain of an empty life. James says highly effective Christians are impartial, rooted in an alliance with Jesus. They are unwavering in their commitment to that friendship. Consequently, they live high-impact lives.

7. Sincere

Finally, a highly effective Christian is sincere. This Greek word was used to describe actors who would use masks so they could change identities throughout the play.

Unfortunately, when Christians fail in this regard, great damage is done to the cause of Christ. We see this in our culture today. In the book *The Day America Told the Truth,* authors James Patterson and Peter Kim report that when a national survey asked respondents to rank various professions for their honesty and integrity, TV evangelists came out almost at the very bottom, below lawyers, politicians, car salesmen, and even prostitutes. Out of the seventy-three occupations compared in the integrity rating, only two ended up lower on the scale: organized crime bosses and drug dealers. No wonder their impact is minimal. Highly effective Christians are people of integrity.

James concludes his thoughts on wisdom in verse 18: "Peacemakers who sow in peace raise a harvest of righteousness." So go and plant seeds of peace that we might raise a harvest of righteousness. How? Ellen White answers: "By honesty and industry, with a proper care of the body, applying every power of the mind to the acquisition of knowledge and wisdom in spiritual things, every soul may be complete in Christ, who is the perfect pattern of a complete man."[30]

10

James 4:1-12

Got Conflict?

Madonna's mad. According to this morning's *USA Today*, the pop star is encountering some turbulence in her high-flying marriage to British director, Guy Ritchie. Reporter Maria Puente writes: "A London tabloid, says she was in tears after a row with Ritchie in a London restaurant this week."[31]

Mind you, Madonna's not the only one in conflict. Consider some other headlines from the same newspaper: "Canada, Brazil duke it out for title of regional jet king"; "Prison for rapper ODB in cocaine case"; "China trade fight lands in House again"; and "Cruise and Cruz are in Fiji, and Kidman is in shock."

Whether you're talking about Tom Cruise, Madonna, or me, it seems that conflict is as customary as the common cold. If you ever interact with people, chances are 100 percent good that you're going to have conflict.

A friend once said to me, "After I graduated from med school, I realized that doctors have to deal with people. So I became an engineer because machines are so much easier to work with. The problem is, even now I get conflict at work because I still have to mess with people."

Indeed, no matter what you do, you have got to mess with people. And that gets messy. It means conflict. So you may as well take notes from James on the vital topic of conflict—its causes and cures.

He begins with an important question: "What causes fights and quarrels among you?" (James 4:1a). Catch a talk show today, and you'll probably catch some fights and quarrels. Whether it's Jerry Springer hosting "Conflicts between betrayed lovers" or Sally refereeing "Sisters at war," or Oprah offering "Dr. Phil's counsel for quarreling couples," it seems everyone's interested in this topic. Rarely, however, do the "experts" on TV back up to ask why there's conflict in the first place. That's where James starts. Then he offers an insightful explanation: "Don't they come from your desires that battle within you?" (James 4:1b). What's causing the rift? Look in the mirror.

Some years ago I heard Pastor Charles Swindoll share the following highlight from a report issued by the Minnesota Crime Commission. It is a statement concerning children in the state of Minnesota. While it does not come from a religious organization, you might jump to that conclusion, based on their statement about humankind. Listen to their assessment:

> Every baby starts life as a little savage. He is completely selfish and self-centered. He wants what he wants when he wants it. His bottle, his mother's attention, his playmate's toy, his uncle's watch. Deny him these and he seethes with rage and aggressiveness, which would be murderous, were he not so helpless.
>
> He is dirty. He has no morals, no knowledge, no skills. This means that all children, not just certain children, but all children are born delinquent. If permitted to continue in the self-centered world of his infancy given free reign to his impulsive actions to satisfy his wants, every child would grow up a criminal, a thief, a killer or a rapist.[32]

That's you and me in the raw. That's the nature that rages within. Therein is the problem—the conflict within. James identifies three of these conflicting desires.

"You want something, but don't get it. You kill and covet, but you cannot have what you want. You quarrel and fight" (James 4:2). The hunger to *have* causes conflicts. "Materialism is organized emptiness of the spirit," says Franz Werfel. "When you want something you can't get," James explains, "there is a dissonance that destroys the soul. This desire to have ignites quarrels and fights."

So how are you doing on this one? Are you inclined to buy into the myth of more? If so, listen to the wisdom of the Word. The desire to have more is an unquenchable thirst. Listen to the story of someone who has been down that road.

> "All he ever wanted was more. He wanted more money, so he parlayed inherited wealth into a billion dollar pile of assets. He wanted more fame, so he broke into the Hollywood scene and soon became a filmmaker and star. He wanted more pleasures, so he paid handsome sums to indulge his every sexual urge. He wanted more thrills, so he designed, built, and piloted the fastest aircraft in the world.
>
> "He wanted more power, so he secretly dealt political favors so skillfully, that two U.S. presidents became his pawns. All he ever wanted was more. He was absolutely convinced that more would bring him true satisfaction. Unfortunately, history shows otherwise. This man concluded his life emaciated, colorless, sunken chest, fingernails in grotesque, inches-long corkscrews, rotting black teeth, tumors, innumerable needle marks from his drug addiction."[33]

Howard Hughes died believing the myth of more—a billionaire junkie, insane by all reasonable standards.

Now if Howard Hughes had pulled off one more deal, made one more million dollars, had one more powerful politician in his hip pocket, would it have been enough? Would it ever have been enough? Somebody asked Howard Hughes once, "How much does it take to make a man happy?"

He said, "Just a little bit more."

"You do not have, because you do not ask God. When you ask, you do not receive, because you ask with wrong motives, that you may spend what you get on your pleasures" (James 4:2, 3).

A self-absorbed life is an invitation to conflict. Spending everything on pleasure inevitably ends in emptiness. Thus James earmarks the desire to feel pleasure as another cause of conflict.

Oscar Wilde's testimony illustrates:

> The gods have given me almost everything. But I let myself be lured into long spells of senseless and sensual ease. . . . I grew careless of the lives of others. I took pleasure where it pleased me, and passed on. I forgot that every little action of the common day makes or unmakes character, and that therefore what one has done in the secret chamber, one has some day to cry aloud from the house-top. I ceased to be lord over myself. I was no longer the captain of my soul, and did not know it. I allowed pleasure to dominate me. I ended in horrible disgrace.[34]

To live with that kind of inner conflict is not to live at all. No wonder James points to the relentless pursuit of pleasure as an avenue of futility.

The final cause of conflict is a desire to fit in the world. James continues:

> You adulterous people, don't you know that friendship with the world is hatred toward God? Anyone who chooses to

> be a friend of the world becomes an enemy of God. Or do you think Scripture says without reason that the spirit he caused to live in us envies intensely? But he gives us more grace. That is why Scripture says: "God opposes the proud but gives grace to the humble" (James 4:4-6).

The third cause of conflict comes when befriending the world. This desire to be embraced by the world compromises the inner peace that God gives to those who are humble. C. S. Lewis nails this notion in *Mere Christianity*:

> God designed the human machine to run on Himself. He Himself is the fuel our spirits were designed to burn, or the food our spirits were designed to feed on. There is no other. That is why it is just no good asking God to make us happy in our own way without bothering about religion. God cannot give us a happiness and peace apart from Himself, because it is not there. There is no such thing.

Simply put, without God conflict reigns.

How then do we quiet this conflict of the soul? What are the cures for conflict?

By now, we've come to expect from James that he will bypass the superficial quick-fix answers and get right at the core. As for conflict resolution James is not happy with external bandages; he insists on going deeper. Mind you, his counsel runs contrary to the way we typically tackle conflict.

For example, consider the case of a man who says, "My marriage is flat. There's constant conflict, and I don't know how much longer we will survive." Being a typical American male he looks to external sources to solve the problem. He reckons there's a seminar or a counselor or a book that can remedy the wreck. After exhausting those resources, he looks for a new wife—another solution that is "out there" somewhere. So he trots down to the divorce court to undo the "I do's." Then he finds a new honey and guess what? Soon the new knot is just as knotted as the old one. That's because his focus has been on external solutions.

Albert Einstein was fond of saying, "The significant problems we face cannot be solved at the same level of thinking we were at when we created them."

In other words, to resolve our problems we must engage in a deeper level of thinking. Rather than searching for external solutions, we must look within. This approach looks inside at principles and character rather than searching for some panacea that exists "out there."

To resolve conflict from the inside means you start with yourself. It suggests that if you want to have a happy marriage, then you must be the kind of person who facilitates a healthy union. If you want to raise a cooperative teenager, then you must be an empathetic, loving, and consistent parent. If you weary of the conflict at work, then you must ask yourself what things you can do to be a better employee. Start there.

This inside-out approach says that private victories precede public victories. Private greatness precedes public greatness. Stephen Covey heralded this principle in his bestseller:

> *Anytime we think the problem is "out there," that thought is the problem.* We empower what's out there to control us. The change paradigm is "outside-in"—what's out there has to change before we can change.
>
> The proactive approach is to change from the inside-out: to *be* different, and by being different, to effect positive change in what's out there—I can *be* more resourceful, I can *be* more diligent, I can *be* more creative, I can *be* more cooperative.[35]

That's how James gets at the cures for conflict. It's all about *being* different on the inside. How? Again, consider three suggestions.

"Submit yourselves, then, to God. Resist the devil, and he will flee from you" (James 4:7).

The first step is submission. Just give it up.

Recall that the cause of conflict rests in the desire to have, feel, and fit in the world. In a word, it's the desire to *control.* I want to control my portfolio, my emotions, my wife, my kids, my colleagues, and my destiny. The result? Conflict. The antidote to this conflict comes in way of surrendering control. Rest in the power of God. The result? The devil is resisted, and he will flee from you. So let go. What does that mean?

To let go is not to care for, but to care about.

To let go is not to fix, but to be supportive.

To let go is not to judge, but to allow another to be a human being.

To let go is not to be in the middle, arranging all the outcomes, but to allow others to affect their own destinies.

To let go is not to deny, but to accept.

To let go is not to nag, scold, or argue, but instead to search out my own shortcomings and correct them.

To let go is not to regret the past, but to grow and live for the future.

To let go is not to cut myself off. It's the realization that I can't control another.

To let go is not to try to change or blame another. It's to make the most of myself.

To let go is to fear less and to love more.[36]

"Come near to God and he will come near to you. Wash your hands, you sinners, and purify your hearts, you double-minded. Grieve, mourn and wail. Change your laughter to mourning and your joy to gloom" (James 4:8, 9).

Our carnal nature is terrifying. Thus James calls us to confession—"Grieve, mourn and wail," he says. If we are to resolve conflict, we must confess who we really are—warts and all.

My favorite story of confession comes from the pen of John Ortberg:

> Some years ago we traded in my old Volkswagen Super Beetle for our first piece of new furniture: a mauve sofa. It was roughly the shade of Pepto-Bismol, but because it represented to us a substantial investment, we thought "mauve" sounded better.
>
> The man at the furniture store warned us not to get it when he found out we had small children. "You don't want a mauve sofa," he advised. "Get something the color of dirt." But we had the naïve optimism of young parenthood. "We know how to handle our children," we said. "Give us the mauve sofa."
>
> From that moment on, we all knew clearly the number one rule in the house. Don't sit on the mauve sofa. Don't touch the mauve sofa. Don't play around the mauve sofa. Don't eat on, breathe on, look at, or think about the mauve sofa. Remember the forbidden tree in the Garden of Eden? "On every other chair in the house you may freely sit, but upon this sofa, the mauve sofa, you may not sit, for in the day you sit thereupon, you shall surely die."
>
> Then came The Fall.
>
> One day there appeared on the mauve sofa a stain. A red stain. A red jelly stain.
>
> So my wife, who had chosen the mauve sofa and adored it, lined up our three children in front of it: Laura, age four, and Mallory, two and a half, and Johnny, six months.
>
> "Do you see that, children?" she asked. "That's a stain. A red stain. A red jelly stain. The man at the sofa store says

it is not coming out. Not forever. Do you know how long forever is, children? That's how long we're going to stand here until one of you tells me who put the stain on the mauve sofa."

Mallory was the first to break. With trembling lips and tear-filled eyes, she said, "Laura did it." Laura passionately denied it. Then there was silence, for the longest time. No one said a word. I knew the children wouldn't, for they had never seen their mother so upset. I knew they wouldn't, because they knew that if they did, they would spend eternity in the time-out chair.

I knew they wouldn't, because *I* was the one who put the red jelly stain on the mauve sofa, and I knew I wasn't saying anything. I figured I would find a safe place to confess—such as in a book I was going to write, maybe.[37]

Truth be told, we all have stained the sofa. There's plenty to confess in all of us. James's appeal to the double-minded sinners to purify their hearts is on target. In so doing, we counter conflict and foster community. Such has been my experience. Whenever I confess "I was wrong. Can you forgive me?" it's like Aloe Vera on a sunburned soul.

Confession is not burping our sins in public so everyone can wince. It is the purifying process through which God allows us to experience His grace. Dietrich Bonhoeffer said it well: "A man who confesses his sins in the presence of a brother knows that he is no longer alone with himself; he experiences the presence of God in the reality of the other person."[38]

James concludes the passage with this challenge: "Humble yourselves before the Lord, and he will lift you up" (James 4:10).

Got conflict? Submit yourself to God, confess your sins, and He will lift you up. So, what are you waiting for?

James 4:13-17

Facing the Future

My gut swirled with giddy anticipation. The opportunity to speak at a youth conference in Sweden painted a smiley face on my spirit. What was supposed to be a mountaintop experience quickly turned into a heart-wrenching valley.

That's because I arrived the morning after the worst fire disaster in the history of Sweden. Because of that, a dark cloud polluted the rally.

Maybe you recall hearing news reports of the Halloween party that exploded into a nightmare. Nearly 400 young people packed into the second floor of a rented warehouse. The booze was flowing. The music was blaring. Everybody was dancing.

According to a local report, the disc jockey was the one who first noticed smoke seeping out of the electrical closet. He started shouting, "Fire! Get out!"

But nobody believed him. Apparently, many kids assumed it was just a Halloween hoax. So because dance floor space was prime real estate, they weren't going to be duped into leaving. So they danced on—until fire engulfed the room.

The only exit quickly clogged, forcing some to leap from second-story windows. Others were trampled in the mayhem. By the time the smoke settled, hundreds of young people landed in local hospitals; sixty-seven perished.

The following afternoon, I visited the site of the catastrophe. Thousands of flowers and candles snaked down the alley from the gutted building. Photographers and newscasters scurried around, scarring the sacredness of the sober moment. Monstrous satellite dishes punctuated the hazy landscape like giant tombstones in a makeshift cemetery. Mourners stood like statues in shock.

A numbness, unlike anything I've ever felt, overwhelmed me. I wept as the woman next to me offered an explanation of her pain. "My son," she sobbed. "It was my son."

To this day the episode seems so surreal. It doesn't seem possible that sixty-seven young people would die at a party. Still, such tragedies happen and remind us all that tomorrow is not promised.

That's what James is driving at in the end of chapter 4. Listen to his counsel:

> Now listen, you who say, "Today or tomorrow we will go to this or that city, spend a year there, carry on business and make money." Why, you do not even know what will happen tomorrow. What is your life? You are a mist that appears for a little while and then vanishes. Instead, you ought to say, "If it is the Lord's will, we will live and do this or that." As it is, you boast and brag. All such boasting is evil. Anyone, then, who knows the good he ought to do and doesn't do it, sins (James 4:13-17).

James wrote during an era when entrepreneurs were busy founding cities. Often the founders were anxious to entice people—particularly Jews—to live in their city. The Jews had a reputation as great traders in the ancient world. Their business savvy could help to ignite a healthy local economy.

So the picture is a familiar one to any Jew who would be reading this letter from James. The example was commonplace of a man randomly pointing to a city on the map and saying, "I'll move there and I can make lots of money. I'll get in on the ground floor and get rich and then come back."

The scenario reminds me of a recent encounter I had while sitting next to an elderly couple on the Hertz shuttle going to O'Hare airport in Chicago. At the first stop the driver announced, "American Airlines." The man grabbed his luggage, kissed the woman goodbye and quipped, "I'll see you when we get there."

I must have looked confused because the woman felt obliged to explain. "That's my husband," she said, "and we're flying to the same place but I tried to book my flight right after we got his and the fare jumped over $500. I waited a day and found a flight on a different airline for $300 cheaper than he paid. So we're flying to the same place but on different airlines."

Feeling the need to continue the conversation, I said, "So where are you going?"

"Orlando," she said. "How about you? Where are you going?"

"I'm flying home to Walla Walla, Washington."

Her jaw dropped. Her eyes swelled to the size of coconuts. "No way!" she gasped. "Are you serious? You're from Walla Walla?"

Now that's not the typical reaction I get when I identify my hometown. Fully expecting her to say that her grandpa invented the Walla Walla sweet onion or her mom named the town, I said, "So you've heard of it?"

"Heard of it!" she gasped, "my husband and I, we've both seen it on a map."

Now she really had me going. "No way!" I said, "you've seen it on a map?"

"Yes, my husband and I took a vacation in Seattle last summer, and we're trying to decide where we want to settle for retirement. So we closed our eyes and pointed on the map. Guess where my finger landed."

"Walla Walla?"

"Bingo! And as soon as we read the name we were convinced that it was a sign from the higher powers of the universe. I mean, Walla Walla—it flows off your tongue. Just the name has an energy to it, like a life-giving force. You must be really proud to tell people you're from Walla Walla."

"Lady," I said, "you have no idea what an egotistical buzz I get every time I say where I'm from. It's like saying my address is the White House." After a brief pause I asked, "So where you from?"

"Oh, we're from Chicago."

My jaw dropped. I said, "No way . . . I've seen it on a map!"

She chuckled then got up to leave. "Well, maybe someday we'll be neighbors in Walla Walla."

To this day I can't imagine landing in a retirement community based on the random pointing method. Yet apparently some folk still do it. James slams the method on the basis that no one can presume on the future. He asserts that life is but a mist that could evaporate by tomorrow.

William Barclay comments: "This uncertainty of life is not a cause either for fear or for inaction. It is a reason for realizing our complete dependence on God. It has always been the mark of a serious-minded man that he makes his plans in such dependence."[39]

The person who fails to do this is guilty of arrogant boasting. The word is *alazoneia.* The word picture associated with this word is that of a wandering quack promoting some panacea that in reality is nothing but a placebo. This person boasts of cures but is unable to deliver.

James makes it clear that such behavior is sin. To know that life is so fragile and yet continue in the self-confident habit of trying to control one's own life is to offend the Author of life. Paul A. Cedar observes: "After identifying the three specific sins, in verse 15 James shares with us a practical formula which we should use in making our plans for the future. This simple and important formula contains one basic contention, 'If the Lord wills, we shall live and do this or that.' "[40] In other words, our focus should always be on doing God's will.

Unfortunately, as we anticipate the future it's not always easy to discern God's will. Over and over I hear the question: "How can I know God's will in my life?" Our chaplain tells me that she fields the question from college students at least once a week. In a recent sermon survey, it was the most requested topic (by a ratio of almost 2 to 1 over the next request). Once again yesterday I got the question while giving a guest lecture in a theology class.

Here's how the question was packaged yesterday: "Ah, Pastor," the student interrupted, "how can I know what God wants me to do after graduation?"

"Tell me your story," I prompted.

"Well, sorry to get off the topic of your lecture, but four years ago I sacrificed a lucrative career in engineering to come to Walla Walla College. At the time a man told me that God revealed to him in a dream that I was to come be his business manager. I asked him why God didn't mention that I had already sent in my deposit to the college. But now that I'm ready to graduate, I have no clue what I'm going to do. I don't know if I can work for the denomination or what. What do you think?"

"Well, um, ah," I stalled for time to collect my thoughts. "I, um, I'm not sure what to tell you."

"I enrolled in college later in life. I thought it was God's calling to ministry, but now I don't know if it was a big mistake or not. I don't know where I'm going to work."

I laid down my lecture notes and responded. "I don't know what to say, other than to tell you my own experience. I took a double major in college because I wasn't sure that working for the denomination would really pan out. Then I did two master's degrees—one in business and one in theology—to make sure I had options. I never dreamed that thirteen years later I would still be a pastor of a local church, but here I am and I love it."

"But maybe my story won't work out like that," he said.

"It may not," I agreed, "but I wonder if sometimes we ask the wrong question. Rather than asking 'How can I know God's will?' I think we should ask 'How can I know God?' "

"What do you mean?"

"Well, when I was trying to decide whether or not to accept a call to pastor in another church, people often asked, 'Do you think God is calling you there?' Frankly, I had a strong sense that God was reassuring me that no matter what decision I made, He could bless me. If I drop out of full-time ministry and become a lawyer or a real estate agent, no doubt I can still please God in those vocations. No matter what my job description, if I continually ask 'How can I know God?' and then pursue that passion, I can live in the center of His will."

"That's very helpful to hear," the student said.

"No matter where you're at next year," I said, "God will ordain you to do His work. No matter who signs your checks, God is wanting you to respond to a higher calling than the world can offer you—whether you're a preacher or a printing-press operator."

At the closing bell, I shared a text and a quote I have found personally helpful in answering the student's question. Romans 12:1, 2 says, "Therefore, I urge you, brothers, in view of God's mercy, to offer your bodies as living sacrifices, holy and pleasing to God—this is your spiritual act of worship. Do not conform any longer to the pattern of this world, but be transformed by the renewing of your mind. Then you will be able to test and approve what God's will is—his good, pleasing and perfect will."

In the words of Lloyd Ogilvie, "The will of God is not a mysterious set of sealed orders we search for and receive if we happen to hit on the right formula. Rather, the will of God is a relationship with Him in which He discloses His purpose, power, and plan for our lives."

Now that's not a bad way to face the future. Just stay in a relationship with Jesus.

12

James 5:1-6

Who *Really* Wants to Be a Millionaire?

I had never met Elizabeth. But because someone heard from a friend of a friend of a friend that I conduct funerals, I got a phone call when Elizabeth died.

"Yes, um, Reverend Haffner, ah," the man stammered. "I'm Bill Moyer. I know you don't know my family or me, um, but we heard you do nice funerals. So we want you to officiate at my wife's service. I'm willing to pay, of course, whatever you charge."

We arranged to meet that afternoon at Bill's home. When I arrived, the butler was waiting at the door with an offer of coffee and an escort to the "sitting parlor." I tried not to gape at the gaudy artwork that decorated the marble hallway.

After passing the water fountain and three yapping poodles, I met Bill. Extending his hand to shake mine, he flashed enough gold to sink a yacht. "Have a seat, Reverend," he said.

"Um, please just call me Karl."

After the customary chitchat, Bill said, "So, what do you need to know about Elizabeth?"

"Well, just tell me about her. What kind of person was she?"

"She loved to shop," he said abruptly.

I wrote it down. "What else?"

"Well, um, ah, let's see . . . she loved to shop."

I underlined what I had already written and kept probing. "OK, and what else?"

"Her passion was shopping."

"Yes, I understand that, but—"

"No," he snapped, "you *don't* understand." He motioned for me to follow him.

I fell in line as he took me to a room that was bigger than the master bedroom in my house. I gawked at a maze of circular garment racks that supported a truckload of silk and price tags. "This was Elizabeth's blouse room. As you can see, most of these she never wore," Bill explained.

Next Bill led me to the "Imelda Marcos room"—which housed enough shoes to outfit a night at the Oscars. Then we hit the "fur room," the "dress room," and finally the "accessories room."

By the end of the tour I got the idea that Elizabeth loved to shop. "Did she support any charities or volunteer somewhere or dote over grandchildren or—" I questioned Bill.

"No," Bill said. "Pretty much all she ever did was shop."

At the funeral only a sprinkling of people occupied the pews. At Bill's request I gave an invitation for people to share their memories of Elizabeth. After a long, awkward gap of silence, one man said, "Well, Elizabeth knew all the sales clerks at Saks Fifth Avenue."

"Yes," another chimed in. "She really liked to shop." Everyone nodded in agreement, and I offered the closing prayer.

The memory of that funeral still haunts me. While there's nothing wrong with shopping, leading a life consumed by hoarding—with no interest in sharing or volunteering or giving back—is to guarantee a funeral at which the unspoken consensus is: *Here lies potential wasted.*

I should say it's a good thing James did not officiate at Elizabeth's funeral. As you might guess, I didn't opt for the following passage for my homily on that occasion.

> Now listen, you rich people, weep and wail because of the misery that is coming upon you. Your wealth has rotted, and moths have eaten your clothes. Your gold and silver are corroded. Their corrosion will testify against you and eat your flesh like fire. You have hoarded wealth in the last days. Look! The wages you failed to pay the workmen who mowed your fields are crying out against you. The cries of the harvesters have reached the ears of the Lord Almighty. You have lived on earth in luxury and self-indulgence. You have fattened yourselves in the day of slaughter. You have condemned and murdered innocent men, who were not opposing you (James 5:1-6).

In verse 1, James issues a stern warning to the rich. After reading it, you have to wonder who *really* wants to be a millionaire. After all, the rich have enormous responsibility. "Weep and wail," James preaches, "because the terror of the judgment will be unleashed upon you." The intensity of his warning is heightened by the word he uses for *wail*. It is the verb *ololuzein*, which is onomatopoeic—it carries its meaning in its sound. It suggests something more than simply wailing. It is a shrieking howl that depicts the horror of the judgment (see Isaiah 13:6; 14:31; 15:2, 3; 16:7; 23:1, 14; 65:14; Amos 8:3).

Even today it's tempting to shrug off James's warning. After all, the judgment seems so far off in the future, right? But beware. The day of judgment is sure. I was reminded of this truth some years ago.

January 1, 3:00 A.M. My wife, Cherié, and I were sleeping off a late-night New Year's Eve party. Suddenly there was a loud, thumping noise downstairs—as if someone were trying to break into our house.

Cherié rolled over and asked groggily, "What's that noise?"

"What noise?" I shouted. (I had to shout to be heard over the loud, thumping noise.)

"I know what it is!" Cherié exclaimed suddenly. "There's some guy loose in the neighborhood—some tattooed, ax-wielding, mouth-foaming, homicidal maniac who escaped from a maximum-security penitentiary for the criminally insane. Go check it out."

"Wait a minute," I protested, "This is the age of equality, you go down."

"I can't! I haven't put on my makeup."

Reluctantly, I stumbled out of bed toward the source of the noise at the front door. I cracked the door just wide enough to observe a very large man.

He thundered, "Are you Mr. Karl Haffner?"

"That depends. Who are you?" I squirmed at him.

"I am here to serve papers to inform you that you are being sued for $20,000 for an accident you were in two years ago." With that, he handed me a stack of papers as thick as my Bible, then vanished into the night. There I stood, clutching a pile of papers.

At that point, I could have dumped the stack in our recycling bin and returned to bed. And when Cherié asked for an explanation, I could have said, "It was nothing. Some drunk pounding on the wrong door."

I *could* have done those things, but that would have been foolish. I knew that the day of judgment—the court date on those papers—would come. So at daybreak (even though it was New Year's Day) I called every one of my attorney friends at home and begged for counsel on how to prepare for my day in court.

As it turned out, on my day of judgment in court, the woman suing me won somewhere in the neighborhood of $14,000. I'll just say that I was very thankful for my insurance company!

The Bible clearly states that someday each of us will face a day of accounting in the heavenly court. Yet I often observe people who drift through life as if they'll never stand before God. They hoard wealth, seemingly oblivious to this impending day.

James goes on to describe the futility of hoarding wealth. "Your wealth has rotted, and moths have eaten your clothes. Your gold and silver are corroded. Their corrosion will testify against you and eat your flesh like fire" (James 5:2-3a).

Again, James chooses vivid wording. For in his culture there were three primary sources of income. First, there was agricultural wealth (corn, grain, and so on) which rots. Second, there was wealth accumulated through garments (Joseph gave garments to his brothers, Naaman brought garments as a gift to the prophet, and in Acts 20:33 Paul claimed that he coveted no man's money or apparel) which are eaten by moths. Finally, there was gold and silver which rusts. The point is that gold and silver do not actually rust; so James is warning the wealthy that even the most secure and indestructible parts of their portfolios will be destroyed.

James punctuates the rundown on wealth with a biting indictment. "You have hoarded wealth in the last days" (verse 3b).

Think about Hetty Green. As a child she became obsessed with money. And as an adult her infatuation with money went beyond obsession.

When Hetty's father died, she inherited $1 million in cash plus $4 million in properties and investments. Carefully she invested her fortune and focused on expanding her financial empire. The sad part is that Hetty's love of money so consumed her that she failed to live a meaningful life.

She feared all conspiracy rumors and was convinced that someone poisoned her father and aunt. And she thought she was next on the hit list. So whenever she traveled she planned obscure routes to confound her enemies.

Rumor has it that she would make up her bed and then sleep underneath it on the floor. That way if anyone broke into her home and tried to kill her, they'd think she was out of town.

When she traveled locally, Hetty rode in a carriage constructed from scrap lumber of an abandoned hen house. For longer trips, she bought a cheap fare and stood in the train's baggage compartment.

Every morning Hetty sent her son to town for a newspaper. After checking the status of her stocks and other investments, she demanded her son return to town to sell the newspaper to someone else.

Every day she ate cold oatmeal. She didn't want to waste the fuel to heat it. And when her son injured his leg, she wasted so much time searching for a free doctor that his leg had to be amputated.

When Hetty died, she left behind an estate valued at nearly $100 million. Her daughter—who was equally as stingy—inherited the whole lot.

Although Hetty Green ranked as one of the richest women in America, she never learned to share with others. She worshipped cash—not Christ. Her master was money. And her life was about getting, not giving. She died very loaded—but very lonely.

In the end, what did it really matter that her bank account had lots of digits (while her son hopped around on one leg thanks to her chintzy heart)? Of what value was her fortune when she died? Or, if you prefer the question the way Jesus would have asked it: "Hetty, what good is it for you to gain the whole world, if you forfeit your soul?" (See Matthew 16:26.)

William Barclay concludes, "It is James's conviction that to concentrate on material things is not only to concentrate on a decaying delusion; it is to concentrate on self-produced destruction."[41] In the end, the true measure of our wealth is how much we'd be worth if we lost all our money.

After making some observations on the worthlessness of riches, James starts meddling (as we'd expect, right?). He levels three in-your-face accusations against the rich. And lest we skim the verses thinking that James is talking only to the Bill Gateses of the world, let me remind you that if you are buying your own home, you're in the top 5 percent of the richest people in the world. By the world's standards most Americans are wildly wealthy. So listen up.

"Look! The wages you failed to pay the workmen who mowed your fields are crying out against you. The cries of the harvesters have reached the ears of the Lord Almighty" (James 5:4).

First, James calls for an honest appropriation of wealth. He condemns the rich who have made their fortunes by ripping off laborers. This practice of stealing from the servants is particularly troubling when you think that the day laborer in Palestine always teetered on the verge of starvation. No farm laborer would have possessed any kind of savings. If his wage was withheld, even for a day, he and his family simply could not eat.

James goes on to challenge the rich to model responsible allocation of wealth. "You have lived on earth in luxury and self-indulgence. You have fattened yourselves in the day of slaughter" (James 5:5). To live in luxury without allocating some resources for the poor is to violate the most basic tenet of Christian faith. It means selling out to a lesser dream than God envisions for you.

Warren Wiersbe, in his book *The Identity Crisis,* makes this insightful observation: " 'The problem is not that money *doesn't* satisfy, but that it *does.* However, it satisfies only those people who are willing to live on a low level where money brings them their greatest happiness.' "[42] To live a self-absorbed life of indulgence is to miss out on a deeper and more meaningful kind of fulfillment. To use James's metaphor, it's as useless as stuffing yourself so you can be fat when you're slaughtered on the day of judgment. That's selling out to a lesser dream.

Finally, James shoots one more stinger toward the rich. He addresses the application of wealth and warns the rich not to abuse it. "You have condemned and murdered innocent men, who were not opposing you" (James 5:6). To accumulate wealth is not a sin. To do so at the expense of innocent people, most certainly is. Such people will go to hell.

I realize that it's politically incorrect to be so blunt, but that doesn't seem to intimidate James. He confronts the wealthy with the way it is.

A news story out of Brooklyn, New York helps to illustrate. Seems a lady got nabbed for speeding. As the officer handed over a citation the woman quipped, "You can go to hell."

The policeman pressed charges, and the woman landed in court to defend her statement. The trial ended with a "Not guilty" verdict. The judge explained, "It wasn't a command or a wish but a statement of fact. For going to hell is a possibility and in fact you can go to hell."

It's true. As James reminds us that you and I can go to hell.

So what do you say that we carefully leverage our resources in a way that honors God? After all, how we spend and save and serve demonstrates what we believe.

James Dobson captured the heart of James's message to the rich in the following parable that I heard recently in a sermon, entitled "It all Goes Back in the Box."

> My grandmother taught me how to play the game Monopoly. Now, my grandmother was a wonderful person. She raised six children. She was a widow by the time I knew her well.
>
> She lived in our house for many, many years. And she was a lovely woman, but she was the most ruthless Monopoly player I have ever known in my life. Imagine what would have happen if Donald Trump had married Leona Helmsley and they would have had a child. Then, you have some picture of what my grandmother was like when she played Monopoly. She understood that the name of the game is to acquire.
>
> When we would play when I was a little kid and I got my money from the bank, I would always want to save it, hang on to it, because it was just so much fun to have money. She spent on everything she landed on. And then, when she bought it, she would mortgage it as much as she could and buy everything else she landed on. She would accumulate everything she could. And eventually, she became the master of the board....
>
> Every time she would take my last dollar, I would quit in utter defeat. And then she would always say the same thing

to me.... "One day, you'll learn to play the game." I hated it when she said that to me.

But one summer, I played Monopoly with a neighbor kid—a friend of mine—almost every day, all day long. We'd play Monopoly for hours.

And that summer, I learned to play the game. I came to understand the only way to win is to make a total commitment to acquisition. I came to understand that money and possessions, that's the the way that you keep score. And by the end of that summer, I was more ruthless than my grandmother. I was ready to bend the rules, if I had to, to win that game.

And I sat down with her to play that fall.

Slowly, cunningly, I exposed my grandmother's vulnerability. Relentlessly, inexorably, I drove her off the board.

The game does strange things to you. I can still remember. It happened at Marvin Gardens. I looked at my grandmother. She taught me how to play the game. She was an old lady by now. She was a widow. She had raised my mom. She loved my mom. She loved me. I took everything she had. I destroyed her financially and psychologically. I watched her give her last dollar and quit in utter defeat.

It was the greatest moment of my life.

And then she had one more thing to teach me. Then she said, "Now it all goes back in the box—all those houses and hotels, all the railroads and utility companies, all that property and all that wonderful money—now it all goes back in the box." I didn't want it to go back in the box. I wanted to leave the board out, bronze it maybe, as a memorial to my ability to play the game.

"No," she said, "None of it was really yours. You got all heated up about it for a while, but it was around a long time before you sat down at the board, and it will be here after you're gone. Players come and players go. But it all goes back in the box."[43]

13

James 5:7-12

Crockpot Christians and Bristlecone Believers

Patience is a virtue.

I know what you're thinking. *Yeah, good, just hurry up and tell me where to get it.*

Well, you can develop patience pretty much anywhere. For example, next time you're waiting for an elevator, try pushing the button only once. Of course this is physically and emotionally impossible even though the Surgeon General has determined that repeatedly pushing the elevator button does not cause the car to think, *Oh my, I best hurry because somebody needs me now.* We still push impatiently, huh?

The grocery store is another place to practice patience. If you're like me, at the checkout you count how many people are in each line then race to the shortest line. If it's a tie, then you carefully count each item in every cart. If it's still a tie, you commit—but not before you note who you would have been in the other line. If that person beats you through line you feel depressed the rest of the day.

You can even develop patience in the kitchen. All you have to do is trash your microwave and crank up the crockpot. That'll give you six days before you steam your beans. In case you're not familiar with the crockpot, it is a round appliance much like any brown mixing bowl. The only difference is that you plug in the crockpot so the food is cooked much slower than room temperature.

As I see it, the only use for a crockpot is to have a metaphor for what Christians ought to be like. In this next passage, James recruits crockpot Christians—that is, disciples of Christ who are marked by the virtue of patience.

Listen to James: "Be patient, then, brothers, until the Lord's coming" (James 5:7). While the word *crockpot* doesn't actually appear in the Greek, that's the idea behind the word *makrothumeo.* It's a combination of two words: "macro," meaning long, and "thermos," meaning heat. In other words it describes someone who takes a long time to get hot.

Notice that James is challenging Christians as opposed to nonbelievers. Four times in this short passage he uses the label "brothers" to address his reading audience. He calls for believers to model the primary attribute of a crockpot—patience.

Next, James uses the farmer to illustrate. Look at verse 7. "See how the farmer waits for the land to yield its valuable crop and how patient he is for the autumn and spring rains" (James 5:7).

One summer I learned the truth of James's words. That's when I discovered the secret to a lush lawn—fertilizer. My yard belonged in a twelve-step group for it was, without question, chemically dependent. The drugs made it look like the eighteenth fairway at Augusta.

Discovering this secret to a green lawn made me as cocky as a farmer in a fruit market. Since I knew the secret, I stopped asking advice. I ignored the landscaper's counsel on the brand and timing and amount of fertilizer. I loaded up on the cheapest stuff and paid no attention to the proportions suggested for optimum results.

After three weeks of waiting to borrow a friend's spreader, my patience was thinning and my lawn was dying. When I finally got the spreader, it didn't work. Frustrated with the delay and anxious to fertilize before vacation, I ripped into the bags of Fred Meyer's Lawn Food and started throwing the granules everywhere.

What harm could fertilizer do? I wondered. *How else can you get green grass fast?*

After a two-week vacation, I was eager to see my yard. Until I saw it.

I stared in disbelief. I started quivering. Then sweating. Then mumbling. "Cherié, tell me it's not so."

"How embarrassing," my wife mumbled in shock. "How did that happen?"

I said, "Ah, um, a comet? Or vandals? Or maybe, the fertilizer."

Have you ever seen a lawn with leprosy? My yard was nothing but splotches of plush green grass accented with brown dots the size of Houston. Interspersed between the dots were half-moons that advertised my technique of spreading.

After a $143 water bill, a $52 aeration fee, and three months of pampering, my lawn was still as ugly as homemade soup! Eventually, with the TLC reserved for Victoria Gardens, my lawn returned to it's former, lush fertility. But it took over a year. There is just no hurrying the laws that govern the farm.

Can you imagine playing at the swimming hole all summer then planting a zillion pumpkin seeds in November? Don't count on any pumpkin pie by Thanksgiving.

James points to the farmer and comments on how patient he must be in order to enjoy the harvest. A good harvest requires the spring and autumn rain, lots of sunshine and most importantly, time and patience. Then James explains why Christians are to develop patience. "You too, be patient and stand firm, because the Lord's coming is near" (James 5:8).

In light of the soon return of Jesus, we are to be patient. Unfortunately, it seems the thought of Jesus' coming is so often the last thing on our minds. I'm reminded of the girl who heard of

Jesus' second coming at church. On the way home she quizzed her mother.

"Mommy," she asked, "do you believe Jesus will come back?"

"Yes."

"Could He come this week?"

"Yes."

"Today?"

"Yes."

"Could He come in the next hour?"

"Yes."

"In a few minutes?"

"Yes, dear."

"Mommy, would you comb my hair?"

Perhaps some of us would make a few last minute changes if we really believed Jesus was coming in a few minutes. Of course our changes would not be about combing our hair, but rather cleansing our characters. So in light of Christ's soon coming, James implores us to pay attention to character issues like patience.

Next, in the context of crusading for crockpot Christians, James incorporates his two favorite topics—first, the tongue and second, perseverance through suffering.

"Don't grumble against each other, brothers, or you will be judged. The Judge is standing at the door!" (James 5:9).

This is vintage James. In his customary, stick-it-in-your-heart style he comes back to the theme we've heard him trumpet before. "Don't grumble about fellow believers," he says. "Watch your tongue or you will face the Judge of the universe."

So ask yourself some questions: Do I tend to have an attitude of grumbling or gratitude? Is my general attitude one of thanksgiving or complaint? Can I find reason to rejoice in all circumstances?

Russian comedian Yakov Smirnoff tells a delightful story about choosing joy over sorrow—in spite of dreadful circumstances. His family arrived as immigrants in New York City. Too poor to buy groceries, they often skipped meals because the cupboards were bare.

Just before Christmas, Yakov landed a stand-up comedy gig that netted him a jackpot of $45! With a smiling heart and a heartfelt smile, he presented the money to his mom. She reverently handled the cash as if it were the Holy Grail. "We have so much for which to be thankful," she exclaimed. "Now we have enough money to buy a turkey, a Christmas tree and one gift for everybody in the family. Wow! What a country!"

When she arrived at the grocery store, however, she discovered the money was missing. Panic zapped her spirit. "Help!" she said to a nearby policeman. "I lost $45! Have you seen my money? It must have dropped out of my pocket. Help me! Please, help me!"

The policeman searched, but eventually resigned himself to the inevitable. "Ma'am, hate to tell you this but you're looking for a hamburger in a lion cage. It's gone."

"Thank you," Mrs. Smirnoff said. "I'll keep looking. And if you happen to find it, please, bring it to this address."

Later, a teenage girl and a garbage man joined in the search. Unfortunately, they too failed to find the fortune. "Thank you. I'll keep looking. And if you happen to find it, please, bring it to this address."

The thought of telling her family felt like fire in the gut. Just as she feared, the family was excitedly awaiting her arrival when she came home—empty-handed. In tears, she reported the tragedy.

It promised to be a very depressing Christmas.

Mrs. Smirnoff, however, refused to succumb to a complaining spirit. "Even though we don't have anything for Christmas," she said to her family, "we will still be thankful for what we have. Remember: you can always choose joy, no matter the circumstances. I'm thankful that we can live in America. Yakov, what are you thankful for?" One by one, each family member shared something for which they were thankful. The very exercise breathed energy and joy into a wounded family.

On Christmas Eve, the doorbell rang. The same policeman who had searched for the money stood in the doorway sporting a 600-watt smile. "You'll never believe what happened!" he said. "I was on duty tonight when I found the envelope of money you lost! It's $45 just like you said."

His news sparked an explosion of excitement in the Smirnoff family. They would celebrate Christmas with food and gifts after all!

Not a half-hour later the doorbell rang again. It was the teenager that had helped search for the money. "You'll never believe what happened!" she said. "I was walking by the place where you lost your money and I found it!" With that, she handed Mrs. Smirnoff $45 and disappeared quicker than an angel.

Fifteen minutes later, the doorbell rang again. This time the garbage man handed Mrs. Smirnoff a wad of cash. "I was collecting garbage in that section of downtown. Wouldn't you know it—I found your money. Merry Christmas."

Mrs. Smirnoff's eyes started to leak as her trembling hand clutched the cash. "In every situation," she sighed, "there is reason to rejoice."

Remember that the next time you're liable to grumble. "Gratitude is a vaccine, an antitoxin, and an antiseptic," claims John Henry Jowett. "As antitoxins prevent disastrous effects of certain poisons and diseases, thanksgiving destroys the poison of faultfinding and grumbling. When trouble has smitten us, a spirit of thanksgiving is a soothing antiseptic."

Even in the face of pain James calls us to a spirit of thankfulness. If you are patient in all circumstances, God will bring about good. James gives an example of this. "Brothers, as an example of patience in the face of suffering, take the prophets who spoke in the name of the Lord. As you know, we consider blessed those who have persevered. You have heard of Job's perseverance and have seen what the Lord finally brought about. The Lord is full of compassion and mercy" (James 5:10, 11).

James uses Job as the poster child on his campaign for Christians to develop this character virtue of patience and perseverance, even in the face of trials. Job went through a series of tragedies and heartbreaks unlike anybody else in human history. He lost his sons and daughters in a freak accident. He lost his livestock, which would be like us losing our complete portfolios, the house, the car—everything. His employees were all killed. Then his body ballooned in boils and he suffered unimaginably, day and night. Just when it looked like things could not possibly get any worse, his loving wife snuggled up to him in bed one night and whispered in his ear, "If I were you, I'd curse God and die."

How's that for encouragement? Naturally, Job wrestled with the heartbreak of it all. He pondered the question "Why?" The thought of bailing on God crossed his mind. But at the end of the day, Job could declare with great conviction, "My God is faithful."

Through all of Job's heartaches, James says, "Look at what the Lord, who is full of mercy and compassion, has brought about."

When you begin to realize how valuable this character trait of patience can be, then you begin to view trials from a different angle. You see them less as an interruption in your quest to lead a cushy life and more as the stuff out of which character is formed. In this way, trials become more of an ally than an enemy.

Some time ago a fascinating article appeared in *Reader's Digest* telling about a most unusual tree called the bristlecone pine. Growing in the western mountain regions, sometimes as high as two or more miles above sea level, these evergreens may live for thousands of years. The older specimens often have only one thin layer of bark on their trunks.

Considering the habitat of these trees, such as rocky areas where the soil is poor and precipitation is rare, it seems inconceivable that they should live so long or even survive at all. The environmental "adversities," however, actually contribute to their longevity. Cells that are produced as a result of these perverse conditions are densely arranged, and many resin canals are formed within the plant. Wood that is so structured continues to live for an extremely long period of time.

Darwin Lambert contends in his article that bristlecone pines in richer conditions grow faster but soon decay and die. The harshness of their surroundings, then, is a vital factor in making them strong and sturdy.

In the same way, Christians mature into the likeness of Christ through adversity and suffering. Scripture teaches, "No discipline seems pleasant at the time, but painful. Later on, however, it produces a harvest of righteousness and peace for those who have been trained by it" (Hebrews 12:11).

Perhaps you're in a season of suffering. Your mother died. Your father's drinking is getting out of control. You suffered a miscarriage. Your coworker robbed you of a promotion you deserve. The tumor is malignant. The divorce proceedings are almost final.

Instead of complaining, claim God's promise that "after you have suffered a little while, [God] will himself restore you and make you strong, firm and steadfast" (1 Peter 5:10).

So what does a crockpot Christian look like today? How about a bristlecone believer? I think Dr. Robertson McQuilkin offers us a contemporary and compelling snapshot. His journey captures all the elements of James's passage. His patience was tested in trial. But he refused to complain. Rather, he leaned into faith.

He writes:

> It has been a decade since that day in Florida when Muriel, my wife, repeated to the couple vacationing with us the story she had told just five minutes earlier. *Funny,* I thought, *that's never happened before*. But it began to happen occasionally.

> Three years later when Muriel was hospitalized for tests on her heart, a young doctor called me aside. "You may need to think about the possibility of Alzheimer's," he said. I was incredulous. *These young doctors are so presumptuous—and insensitive.*[44]

Dr. McQuilkin describes the long and slow descent of his wife as she was forced to give up one thing after another—her radio ministry, her speaking career, her writing, and her counseling. Although Muriel was oblivious to what was happening, for Dr. McQuilkin it was a slow death to watch his vibrant, creative, articulate wife gradually dimming out. He describes his struggle:

> She is such a delight to me. I don't *have* to care for her. I *get* to. One blessing is the way she is teaching me so much—about love, for example, God's love. She picks flowers outside—anyone's—and fills the house with them.
>
> Lately she has begun to pick them *inside,* too. Someone had given us a beautiful Easter lily, two stems with four or five lilies on each, and more to come. One day I came into the kitchen and there on the window sill over the sink was a vase with a stem of lilies in it. I've learned to "go with the flow" and not correct irrational behavior. She means no harm and does not understand what should be done, nor would she remember a rebuke. Nevertheless, I did the irrational—I told her how disappointed I was, how the lilies would soon die, the buds would never bloom and *please* do not break off the other stem.
>
> The next day our youngest son, soon to leave for India, came from Houston for his next-to-last visit. I told Kent of my rebuke of his mother and how bad I felt about it. As we sat on the porch swing, savoring each moment together, his mother came to the door with a gift of love for me: she care-

> fully laid the other stem of lilies on the table with a gentle smile and turned back into the house. I said simply, "Thank you." Kent said, "You're doing better, Dad!"
>
> Muriel cannot speak in sentences now, only in phrases and words, and often words that make little sense: "no" when she means "yes," for example. But she can say one sentence, and she says it often. "I love you."
>
> She not only says it; she acts it. The board arranged for a companion to stay in our home so I could go daily to the office. During those two years it became increasingly difficult to keep Muriel home. As soon as I left, she would take out after me. With me, she was content; without me, she was distressed, sometimes terror stricken. The walk to school is a mile round trip. She would make that trip as many as ten times a day. Sometimes at night, when I helped her undress, I found bloody feet. When I told our family doctor, he choked up. "Such love," he said simply. Then, after a moment, "I have a theory that the characteristics developed across the years come out at times like these." I wish I loved God like that—desperate to be near him at all times. Thus she teaches me, day after day.[45]

The time came when Dr. McQuilkin had to decide between his career and caring for his wife. For him it was an easy decision to make. After all, she had shown him such perfect devotion for forty-two years and now he was glad to keep his promise, "in sickness or in health, till death do us part."

Dr. McQuilkin concludes: "As I watch her brave descent into oblivion, Muriel is the joy of my life. Daily I discern new manifestations of the kind of person she is, the wife I always loved. I also see fresh manifestations of God's love—the God I long to love more fully."[46]

James concludes the passage by saying, "Above all, my brothers, do not swear—not by heaven or by earth or by anything else.

Let your 'Yes' be yes, and your 'No,' no, or you will be condemned" (James 5:12).

This verse is a good reminder that you can choose. Patience in suffering? It's your choice. Controlling your grumbling? Again, you choose. It's your choice to love your spouse until the finish line. You decide if you want to be a crockpot Christian.

If you think about it, your entire life is defined by two words: yes and no. So James underscores how important these two words can be.

Even though these two words are crucially important, we often use them casually. And then sometimes we have a problem saying the right one at the right time. Occasionally, too, we just give in to the pressure of the moment—even though our pressured decisions may not lead us in the direction of our ultimate beliefs and values.

Somebody asks, "Would you baby-sit my hyperactive, insomniac triplets while my husband and I move to Kentucky?"

"Would you go on a blind date with my cousin this Sunday . . . when he gets out of prison?"

"Would you take my homemade airplane for a spin to see if it works?"

Although you had a decisive "No!" in your mind, much to your surprise it's "Yes" that jumps up your throat and slides out your mouth.

Jesus alluded to the importance of these two words when He said, " 'Simply let your "Yes" be "Yes," and your "No," "No"; anything beyond this comes from the evil one' " (Matthew 5:37). Jesus taught that the correct use of these two words would define your life and determine your legacy.

This idea flies in the face of the popular illusion that "my life is not chosen by me. It's beyond my control. I am just a victim of twisted parents and dysfunctional teachers."

Rubbish! The Bible teaches that you—and only you—are responsible for your life. What you sow, you reap. If your way of life is damaging your heart and your soul, nobody's going to fix that for you. Yep, you're crafting your life by saying "Yes" or "No" to money commitments, relational choices, job opportunities, family requests, interruptions, what you'll watch on TV, which parties you'll attend, and how you'll treat people. This is the power of yes and no.

Jesus was a master at this. When the Father asked Him to become a human being in order to save lost folk, Jesus said, "Yes!" When a leper said to Jesus, "If You are willing, You can make me clean." He said, "Yes!" At the climax of His life when He was in the Garden of Gethsemane, He prayed, "God, I so desperately want to say no to drinking from this cup, but because the redemption of the human race is hinging on My answer, I will say yes."

But Jesus also knew when to say no. When Satan said, "If You are really the Son of God, take a flying leap off this mountain," Jesus said, "No!" When good friends approached Him with a misguided request—"Jesus, let us sit next to You, one on Your right and one on Your left so we can be the hotshots in heaven"—Jesus said, "No!" When an overzealous disciple whacked off a man's ear, suggesting that physical force might be the best defense, Jesus said, "No!"

Jesus had great clarity about His identity, His passion, and His purpose. His "Yes" was "Yes" and His "No" was "No." Thus He lived with great freedom.

Now just imagine living with that kind of clarity about who God made you to be. Imagine living with that kind of resolve in your marriage, at work, and at home. The fact is, you can. You decide. It's as simple as yes and no.

14

James 5:13-20

Practically Praying

It was a simple deal. Roxanne would give the canvass, and I would pray.

She began her presentation. "Mrs. Olson, in just thirty minutes I'll show you how *Uncle Arthur's Bedtime Stories* and *Bible Stories* can help you spiritually train your children . . ."

I began my prayer. *Dear heavenly Father, give Roxanne the words. Open Mrs. Olson's mind to see the value in . . .*

My eyelids felt like bags of books. Roxanne's familiar words were as soothing as a lullaby.

Suddenly Roxanne's familiar question disturbed me like a nightmare. "Which payment plan would work out best for you?"

I jerked awake with the grace of a camel on ice-skates. I quickly moved my leg to cover the drool spot I'd left on the sofa. Roxanne glanced in my direction with a glare that could have burned a hole through a safe.

"What were you doing?" Roxanne screamed after we got in the car.

"Sorry," I said, squirming. "I, ah, was snoozing," I added sheepishly.

"No, you dweeb! It was worse."

"I know, I um, was drooling."

"No!" she shouted. "Worse! For a half hour you were sprawled out on this stranger's couch—*snoring!*"

I must admit that many of my prayers started with good intentions but ended in a nightmare. Maybe you too have struggled with prayer. If so, don't despair. James offers some helpful counsel.

> Is any one of you in trouble? He should pray. Is anyone happy? Let him sing songs of praise. Is any one of you sick? He should call the elders of the church to pray over him and anoint him with oil in the name of the Lord. And the prayer offered in faith will make the sick person well; the Lord will raise him up. If he has sinned, he will be forgiven. Therefore confess your sins to each other and pray for each other so that you may be healed. The prayer of a righteous man is powerful and effective.
>
> Elijah was a man just like us. He prayed earnestly that it would not rain, and it did not rain on the land for three and a half years. Again he prayed, and the heavens gave rain, and the earth produced its crops.
>
> My brothers, if one of you should wander from the truth and someone should bring him back, remember this: Whoever turns a sinner from the error of his way will save him from death and cover over a multitude of sins (James 5:13-20).

First notice the structure of this passage. James builds a pyramid of reasoning that supports his thesis. Not only does he build up to his thesis, but he supports it coming down on the other side as well. Look at it closely.

In verse 13 James asks if any one is in trouble. Let's call that point A. Then point B (verse 13) is the question, "Is anyone happy?" Point C (verse 14) is a third question: "Is any one of you sick?" These questions are all building to the thesis in verse 16: "The prayer of a righteous man is powerful and effective."

The point is that prayer works. To further support this contention, James completes the line of reasoning by echoing points A, B, and C by way of illustrations.

Graphically, the pyramid of logic would look like this:

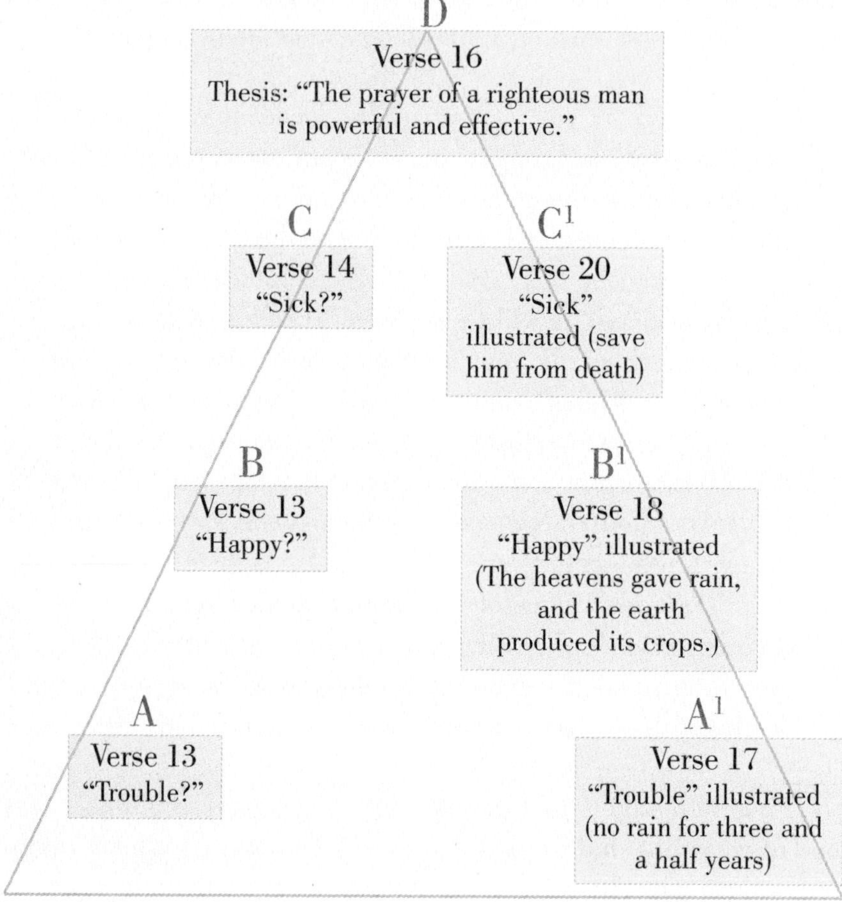

No doubt, according to Scripture, prayer works. But what does that mean? Does it follow then that we should expect to get what we pray for? Is prayer a way to punish our enemy by having God withhold rain? Or by prayer can we turn on the faucets of heaven? Can we really expect healing through prayer? To read the closing verses of James, one might so conclude.

Some years ago, the media reported the story of a man in Florida who prayed for something and didn't get it. So you know what he did? He sued his pastor.

The pastor had preached a sermon based on the text, "Cast thy bread upon the waters." He urged the congregation to pray boldly, assuring them that in return, God would give them prosperity.

So the man made a large contribution to the church, praying that God would reward him accordingly. Well, his business went bankrupt, and he took his pastor to court for false preaching! The case was thrown out of court, and the man was instructed to take the sermons and Scripture less literally.

Is that our problem? Should we simply take James less literally? Can we really defend the thesis that prayer works?

So often we pray believing that if we don't get what we ask for, our prayer didn't "work." But then we make God into a Santa Claus, someone we approach with a wish list. When our wishes are denied, we question the value of prayer.

James makes it clear in verse 15 that prayer can result in healing and forgiveness. We read the command to anoint those who are sick with the promise that "the prayer offered in faith will make the sick person well."

I could fill a book of miraculous results from anointing services that I have done. I think of a two-year-old girl that drowned in a half-frozen lake. She was submersed for over twenty minutes before they recovered her body. Paramedics airlifted her from the remote camp and transported her to the hospital where I performed an anointing. After countless surgeries and several weeks in the hospital, the girl survived with no brain damage. Today she is healthy and happy. Or I could tell you about a close friend who survived a massive heart attack. I don't believe it's merely coincidental that his recovery occurred simultaneously with a prayer meeting where our church family gathered to claim the promise in James 5:15. As recent as last month I facilitated another anointing service for a woman who was given a week to live. Her body has been devoured by cancer. The doctors claimed there was nothing they could do. So she called me as a last resort to anoint her and pray for healing. According to the most recent report her cancer has gone into remission! No doubt, there are numerous stories that testify of the truth of which James writes. (Believe me, it's tempting to fill up the rest of this chapter with those happy stories and be done with it.)

To be fair, however, I must share the full story. Truth is, I could also fill a book of stories that seem to undermine the power of prayer. I think of the anointing service we did for a baby born six weeks premature. We buried her three days later. I also feel obligated to report that my friend who survived the heart attack died less than three months later in a car accident. Another anointing service comes to mind that we did for a young woman plagued by migraine headaches. In spite of our prayers, her anguish continues. So what do I do with all of those stories? To simply share the anecdotes that make God look good is less than honest. Furthermore it undermines the credibility of Christianity with nonbelievers.

If James is right that "the prayer of the righteous man is powerful and effective," then why does God seemingly ignore so many prayers? Why don't I always get what I pray for?

There are lots of answers to that question, most of which are problematic, resulting in shame and hopelessness. You didn't get what you prayed for because . . .

You don't even have the faith of a mustard seed.

There is too much sin in your life.

God knows what is best for you better than you do.

Somebody more spiritual is making the opposite request of God.

Prayer doesn't really work.

There is no God.

If we don't like any of those answers then we must change our understanding of what it means to pray, and what it means for God to answer our prayers.

The Talmud, the collection of ancient rabbinical writings about Jewish Law, offers examples of what prayer does *not* mean. For example, it is not a magic formula for manipulating certain events in life. For a pregnant woman to pray "Please make this baby a boy" is a misguided prayer. The gender of a child is determined at conception, so there is no reason to plead with God to change it. Another example the Talmud gives of a prayer that should not be prayed is when a house is on fire. To approach the neighborhood and see the smoke then utter the prayer "Help it not to be my house" is not only mean-spirited against the neighbor but it is futile. Regardless of how sincere or articulate a prayer might be, whatever house is on fire is simply the way it is.

Similar to the Talmudic cases is the student that prays before opening a letter that it will be an acceptance to medical school. Either it is or it isn't and at that point a prayer is not going to change the letter inside. We cannot ask God to go back and rewrite the past. Nor can we expect God to rewrite the laws of nature to accommodate our immediate desires and needs.

So how should we respond when God seems to disrupt the laws of nature and remove the cancer or revive a drowning victim? I like Rabbi Harold Kushner's answer: "When miracles occur, and people beat the odds against their survival, we would be well advised to bow our heads in thanks at the presence of a miracle, and not think that our prayers, contributions or abstentions are what did it. The next time we try, we may wonder why our prayers are ineffective."[47]

But God did say, "Ask, and you will receive." And He promised a cup overflowing with blessings. So shouldn't we expect results?

Absolutely. But the results usually come in way of God working through personal transformation rather than through abrupt intervention. Instead of changing the letter in the sealed envelope that comes from the medical school, God might choose to change the student's understanding of the outcome. If the letter is a rejection, perhaps the student will learn invaluable lessons of what it means to grow through pain, what trusting God means when He feels far away, what thorough study and preparation is all about, and so on.

In other words, effective prayer results in a person acting more like God. Where we can manifest the will of God, we must do so rather than simply praying for Him to intervene on our behalf. I think James would like this emphasis on being a doer of the prayer whenever it lies in our power to do so.

Consider these words:

> We cannot merely pray to You, O God, to end starvation;
> For you have already given us the resources
> With which to feed the entire world
> If we would only use them wisely.
>
> We cannot merely pray to you, O God,
> To root our prejudice,
> For You have already given us eyes
> With which to see the good in all men
> If we would only use them rightly....
>
> We cannot merely pray to You, O God, to end disease,
> For you have already given us great minds with which
> To search out cures and healing,
> If we would only use them constructively.
>
> Therefore we pray to You instead, O God,
> For strength, determination, and willpower,
> To do instead of just to pray,
> To become instead of merely to wish.[48]

What good, then, is prayer if it is no guarantee for a future spouse or a miraculous cure or something else on your wish list?

Again, Harold Kushner answers:

> Prayer is not a matter of coming to God with our wish list and pleading with Him to give us what we ask for. Prayer is first and foremost the experience of being in the presence of God. Whether or not we have our requests granted, whether or not we get anything to take home as a result of the encounter, we are changed by having come into the presence of God. A person who has spent an hour or two in the presence of God will be a different person for some time afterward.[49]

When we discover the art of living in the presence of God, our circumstances may not change, but our perspective does. Prayer helps us see we are not alone. Prayer helps us define success beyond human terms.

Thus our prayer will not be "Give me a new car because I deserve it" or "I need a promotion at work" or "Make my mother easier to live with." Rather, our prayer will sound like that of the psalmist: "But as for me, it is good to be near God" (Psalm 73:28).

This kind of prayer is the stuff of transformation. No wonder James punctuates his book with a call to prayer. As we have seen, James's argument all along has been that if God is doing a work in us then we must do God's work. If we are truly transformed then we will live transformed lives. How then does this kind of a transformed life happen? Through prayer.

" 'Prayer—secret, fervent, believing prayer—lies at the root of all personal godliness,' "[50] writes William Carey. Richard Foster adds: "To pray is to change. Prayer is the central avenue God uses to transform us. If we are unwilling to change, we will abandon prayer as a noticeable characteristic of our lives. The closer we come to the heartbeat of God the more we see our need and the more we desire to be conformed to Christ."[51]

"To be conformed to Christ"—that's the whole point, isn't it? How can this happen?

Just pray.

15

Living Proof

When the Crystal Palace Exhibition opened in 1851, people flocked to London's Hyde Park to gawk at the latest and the greatest inventions. One of the greatest marvels back then was steam. People stood amazed at the steam plows, steam locomotives, steam looms, steam organs, even a steam cannon.

Of all the exhibits that year, the first-prize winner was a steam invention with 7,000 parts. When the operator turned it on, its pulleys, whistles, bells, and gears made a lot of noise, but, ironically, the contraption didn't do a thing! Seven thousand moving parts making a lot of commotion . . . but having no practical use.

It's easy to confuse activity with accomplishment, to be fooled into thinking that the sound of gears and pulleys is the sound of something important being done.

Is that true of your life? True of your church? Are there hundreds, even thousands, of parts spinning and turning and making a lot of noise, but accomplishing very little?

Be careful, because what you think has substance may dissipate like steam on the day of judgment.

God calls you to be a high-impact player for His kingdom. He doesn't need Christians who yap the right lines but do not yield the right lives. He needs living proof. God's church is not a sauna for Christians blowing off steam. His church is a workout center for followers committed to sweat, service, and spiritual growth.

Put another way, His church is a health club of fully devoted disciples who live the key verse of James: "But someone will say, 'You have faith; I have deeds.' Show me your faith without deeds, and I will show you my faith by what I do" (James 2:18). Genuine followers of Christ understand that faith is a verb.

As we conclude our journey through the book of James, let's recap the major ideas that have emerged. This overview reminds us that God detests sauna spirituality. He calls us to get out of the hot tub and into the world. A review of James's favorite themes makes that clear.

Hands-on Faith

First, James is not content for believers to just hear the truth. He wants us to do it. He contrasts fake faith (claims without conduct) with the real thing. A commitment to serving others signifies authentic faith.

Opportunities to serve abound. Eldon Wallmeyer learned this when he tried to buy a candy bar in a downtown Seattle convenience store last week. But when he emptied his pockets, he found only fifty-two cents.

The clerk said, "Sorry. You need sixty cents."

Wallmeyer put the candy bar back and left. A block away, he was hustled by a panhandler who asked, "Could you spare a dollar?"

Wallmeyer broke into laughter.

The hustler demanded, "What's funny?"

Wallmeyer said it was amusing being asked for a dollar when he didn't have quite enough money for a candy bar.

"How much do you need?" asked the hustler.

Wallmeyer said he was about a dime short.

The hustler reached into his pocket and handed over a coin. "Here," he said to Wallmeyer. "Take this."

Funny, isn't it? How we often stand around as "takers," only to discover that others have bigger needs than we do. And in meeting others' needs, we discover a greater joy in giving than in receiving.

So why not meet these needs today? Why not attack life with a heart ready to serve, hands willing to help, and a life poised to give? Why not live the words of Jesus: "Whoever serves me must follow me. Then my servant will be with me everywhere I am. My Father will honor anyone who serves" (John 12:26, EB)?

When Jesus calls us to serve, He expects us to get our hands dirty, our pockets empty, and our hearts full. That's what James has been telling us all along. Faith is not an intellectual assent to doctrinal beliefs. It is hands-on. It thinks about the needs of others then seeks to meet those needs.

In the following poem, I think Marion Runge aptly summarizes the dream that James holds out for all Christians.

> *If I could have one wish, only a temporary one—*
>
> I would turn those who mistreat animals into one. Let them feel the blow of a shoe, be thrown against a wall; let them be half-frozen, half-starved, and half-dead. Let them be trapped by a foot in the scorching sun or freezing rain; Let them be jabbed by a stick, hit with rocks, swung by the tail. Let them be cornered, chased, frightened, bruised, and left bleeding by horrendous torture.
>
> Then when they return to humans again they will be more tender and kind.
>
> *If I could have another wish, only a temporary one—*
>
> I would make all egotists into frightened, stuttering "wallflowers." Let them be timid and afraid to brag. Let them be pushed out of grocery lines and shoved off bus seats. Let them

miss out on the last item on the bargain table because they were pushed aside. Let them have fear to speak up and lose out on a job promotion because of someone who is not afraid to assert himself. Let them listen, let them wait, let them learn.

Then when they return to their normal self they will be more humble.

If I could have another wish, only a temporary one—

I would wish all skinny people to grow fat, uncomfortably so, gaining day after day, fighting back the tears as the pounds count up. Let them diet on "rabbit food," low carbohydrates, banana-milk, egg-grapefruit, or liquid diets. Let them leave the table with stomachs growling, while others eat chocolate pie. Let them feel the hurt of mockery, snide remarks, "fat" jokes, laughter, and ridicule. Let them feel depressed as they struggle to lose one pound and gain two the next day. Let them feel hopeless, helpless, unloved, and unwanted as they go through life.

When they return to their normal self they will be more sensitive to those who cry inside.

If I could have another wish, only a temporary one—

I would wish a "fruit-basket upset" of skin color and nationalities. Let those who poke fun at ethnics feel the hurt of Polish jokes, Black jokes, Whitey jibes, slanty-eye stories, and jokes about Jews. Let them be outcasts because they are different.

Then when they return to their original color and nationality they will express only kindness.

If I could have another wish, only a temporary one—

I would wish all beautiful people to turn ugly. Let them cry as they look in a mirror and see freak marks of sin, ugly burns, moles, and disfigurement. Let people stare and snicker at them. Let them be left out of circles of friends, unwanted by the opposite sex. Let them feel loneliness.

Then when they are beautiful again they will be less vain.

If I could have another wish, only a temporary one—

I would wish all rich people to become poor. Let their stomachs cry out with hunger pangs. Let them pray for a crust of bread. Let their toes be numb from icy, torn shoes. Let their children be ridiculed for tattered clothes. Let rats nibble on their babies' fingers and toes. Let them feel unloved and desperate.

Then when they are rich again they will be more sensitive to the needs of others.

If I could have another wish, only a temporary one—

I would turn the clock ahead for young people and make them old. Let them hobble because of stiff joints, let them walk a little slower and eat a little longer. Let them be lonely and shut in from the world, especially on holidays. Let them have only memories, but no love. Let them be frightened by young prowlers, beaten by young thieves.

Then when they are young again, they will be more considerate of senior citizens.

If I could have just one wish, a permanent one—

I would wish that everyone would follow the second great commandment, loving his neighbor as himself, with compassion and sensitivity. Then there would be no hurts or tears, no loneliness or fear.

This last wish will come true! Jesus is coming soon.[52]

Trials

The second re-emerging theme is the call to persevere in trials. Because James wrote to Jewish Christians that were scattered throughout the Mediterranean world because of persecution, he hammered a topic that was relevant to his readers. Of course the topic is still as applicable today. In the Christian life there are hardships and temptations. Remaining faithful to Christ through these adversities produces maturity and strong character.

One of the most tragic events during Ronald Reagan's presidency was the Sunday morning terrorist bombing of the Marine barracks in Beirut. Hundreds of Americans were killed or wounded as they slept. For days, stunned survivors worked to dig out the victims from beneath the rubble.

A few days after the tragedy, Marine Corps Commandant Paul Kelly visited some of the wounded survivors in a Frankfurt, Germany, hospital. Among the most severely wounded was Corporal Jeffrey Lee Nashton. He had so many tubes running in and out of his body that a witness said he looked more like a machine than a man. Nevertheless, he survived.

As Kelly neared him, Nashton, struggling to move and racked with pain, motioned for a piece of paper and a pen. He wrote a brief note and passed it back to the commandant.

On the slip of paper were two words—"*Semper Fidelis,*" the Latin motto of the Marines. It means "Ever Faithful." With those two simple words Nashton spoke for the millions of Americans who have sacrificed body and limb and their lives for their country—those who have remained faithful.

Throughout history similar stories of faithfulness abound. And we can find not only stories of loyalty to a country, but also stories of faithfulness to Christ. For example, during China's Boxer Rebellion of 1900, insurgents captured a mission station and blocked all the gates but one. In front of that one gate they placed a cross flat on the ground.

Then the word was passed to the captives that any who trampled the cross underfoot would be permitted their freedom and life, but any refusing would be shot.

Terribly frightened, the first seven captives trampled the cross under their feet and were allowed to go free. But the eighth captive, a young girl, refused to commit the sacrilegious act. Kneeling beside the cross in prayer for strength, she then arose and moved carefully around the cross. She went out to face the firing squad. Strengthened by her example, every one of the remaining ninety-two captives followed her to the firing squad, dying "ever faithful."

While forms of persecution like sizzling at the stake or being crucified upside down are rare in our culture, the battle between right and wrong still rages with a tornado tempo. Being always faithful in today's world isn't easy. Yet the calling of Christ has never changed. " 'If anyone would come after me,' " Jesus once said, " 'he must deny himself and take up his cross daily and follow me. For whoever wants to save his life will lose it, but whoever loses his life for me will save it' " (Luke 9:23, 24).

The book of James has sounded a clarion call for you and me to be always faithful. "To take up the cross," James would argue, "means unswerving obedience even in the face of hardship."

Love

A third theme in the book of James calls us to love. Keeping the law of love demonstrates one's faith. Unless love manifests itself in tangible ways, it cannot be genuine love.

A professor of psychology had a reputation in his neighborhood for giving unsolicited counsel to parents on how to raise their children—even though he had no children of his own. Whenever the professor saw a neighbor scolding a child for some wrongdoing, he would bark, "Ah, ah, ah, ah, ah! You should love your child. Don't punish your kid. Just love, love, love. Be patient with kids, never scold them harshly . . ."

One hot summer afternoon the professor was doing some repair work on a concrete driveway leading to his garage. After several hours of work in the scorching sun he laid down his tools, wiped the perspiration from his forehead, and started toward the house. Just then out of the corner of his eye he saw a mischievous little boy putting his foot into the fresh cement. He rushed over, grabbed him, and preached like a peeved Judge Judy. "You good-for-nothing lousy little—"

Just then a neighbor leaned over the fence and said, "Ah, ah, ah, ah, ah! Remember, Professor! Love, love, love—just love the child."

At this, he yelled back furiously, "I do love him . . . in the abstract but not in the concrete!"

I think all Christians are good at loving in the abstract. Who would dare argue with Jesus when He declared that Christians are to be known by their love? (See John 13:34, 35.) Christ taught that your spirituality is directly proportional to your capacity to love. If you fail to love then you are hallucinating about the value of your religion. So then, how do we live loving lives? Here's a list to start you thinking. I adapted it from a talk I heard years ago by Pastor Bill Hybels at a church leadership conference. Give these a shot then get creative and try some new ways on your own.

1. Say it.

Arguably the three most powerful words are: "I love you." When these words wind their way into any relationship, everything gets redefined. For example, let's say you find someone who makes your heart beat fast. So you start dating. Then comes that heart-thumping moment after a date when you have to say something. So you blush and stammer, "Um, ah, I really enjoy being with you."

If the courtship keeps going, a few weeks later you might say, "I think about you all the time." Later you say, "You're becoming the most important person in my life."

But all that is precursor for the big one. You're just waiting for the moment when the whole relationship gets redefined and someone finally offers, "I love you." When that happens, everything changes.

Of course, verbally expressing love isn't limited to romantic encounters. By sharing words of love you can change the relational DNA at work, at home, and at church. So take a risk today and venture to say words of love.

2. Write it.

Hebrews 3:13 reminds us to "encourage one another daily." I've discovered that a simple note can make a profound impact. For example, I once scribbled a note of affirmation to a friend. Several years later I was surprised to see that it was displayed on my friend's refrigerator. What took me three minutes to write was still life giving after years.

3. Offer an appropriate touch.

A volunteer tells of going to work with Mother Teresa in the streets of Calcutta to serve the poorest of the poor. Upon arrival, Mother Teresa began a tour of their children's home. The tour was interrupted when some workers brought in a baby that they had rescued off the streets. It was apparent that the child would not survive the day. Mother Teresa picked up the baby, handed it to the new volunteer and said, "We'll finish our tour later. For now, do not let this baby die without having been loved."

The volunteer later wrote: "I held that baby in my arms and I loved her until she died at six o'clock in the evening. I spent the hours humming a Brahms lullaby. And you know, I could feel that baby as tiny and as weak as she was, I could feel that baby pressing herself against me."

Even a dying infant responds to human touch.

4. Render acts of kindness.

The apostle John writes: "My little children, let us not love in word, neither in tongue; but in deed and in truth" (1 John 3:18, KJV).

Every act of kindness is an act of love. When you flash a smile to a child or volunteer at a community center or visit someone in the hospital or slip a note to a hurting friend or send a flower, you are doing a small act of kindness as unto the Lord. Your expression of love is small but it's not insignificant.

Wise speech

Another theme that weaves its way through the book of James is the importance of wise speech. We are responsible for the destructive results of our talk. Only by God's wisdom can we control the tongue.

Aesop, the ancient storyteller, told this fable: Once upon a time, a donkey found a lion's skin. He tried it on, strutted around, and frightened many animals. Soon a fox came along, and the donkey tried to scare him, too. But the fox, hearing the donkey's voice, said, "If you want to terrify me, you'll have to disguise your bray." Aesop's moral: Clothes may disguise a fool, but his words will give him away.

We've heard as much from James, haven't we? Our words can define or defy our wisdom.

Pianist Artur Rubenstein, loquacious in eight languages, once told this story on himself when he was assailed by a stubborn case of hoarseness. The newspapers were full of reports about smoking and cancer; so he decided to consult a throat specialist. " 'I searched his face for a clue during the 30 minute examination,' Rubenstein said, 'but it was expressionless. He told me to come back the next day. I went home full of fears, and I didn't sleep that night.'

"The next day there was another long examination and again an ominous silence. 'Tell me,' the pianist exclaimed. 'I can stand the truth. I've lived a full, rich life. What's wrong with me?'

"The physician said, 'You talk too much.' "[53]

Lesson learned? Be quick to listen and slow to speak.

Wealth

The final theme in the book of James concerns wealth. James warned Christians not to adopt a worldly attitude about wealth. Because the glory of wealth fades, Christians are called to store up treasures in heaven through selfless service. Furthermore, Christians are not to show favoritism to the rich or prejudice against the poor. In sum, we are all accountable for how we use what we have.

A fable is told in India of a poor beggar who lived in a state ruled by a Maharaja. The beggar had no home and slept on a mat in a homeless shelter. On frigid evenings he covered himself with a treasured collection of tattered rags.

Having no means of earning a livelihood other than begging, he ventured out every morning. He would sit by the sidewalk with his beggar's bowl as passersby threw some grains of rice or copper coins his way.

Usually he got enough rice for two meals a day. And when he hit the jackpot, he'd also score enough money to buy sticks for a fire and a few vegetables, fish, or dhall for curry.

One day he heard that the Maharaja would be coming his way the following day. The beggar's spirits soared, for he reasoned, *The Maharaja will not give me a handful of rice or a copper coin, but nothing less than gold.*

The next day he awaited the Maharaja's arrival. All day he blistered in the sun, anticipating his good fortune. Finally, at sunset the regal chariot arrived.

Stepping into the road, the beggar brought the chariot to a standstill. He approached the Maharaja and begged for alms. Instead of giving him gold, however, the Maharaja extended his hands and asked the beggar to give him something!

Extremely disappointed that a wealthy ruler would filch from the poor, the beggar counted five grains of rice from his bowl and placed them angrily in the hands of the Maharaja.

"Thank you," the ruler said and continued his journey.

With a sore heart, the beggar returned to the shelter, took out his winnowing fan and began to clean his rice for supper. Yet as he cleaned, he spotted a small glittering object among the rice. Picking it up, he saw that it was a grain of gold. He laid it carefully to one side and went on winnowing until he found another glittering golden grain, then another.

That's when the truth hit him: five grains of rice given to the Maharaja had brought him in return five grains of gold.

"What a fool I was!" he exclaimed regretfully. "If I had known, I'd have given it all to him."

Jesus once taught a similar parable when He urged His followers to invest in the treasures of heaven rather than the treasures of earth. James borrows from that parable and warns that worldly treasures are easily swiped by moths or rust. In contrast, heavenly treasures will always yield a profitable return—if not in this world, certainly in the next.

So why not make a risky deposit today? Give lavishly. Serve wholeheartedly. Love generously. Give the best you have away. But don't worry, someday it will all come back to you in gold.

Do it!

Perhaps the entire book of James is best summarized in two words: Do it! In closing, James would no doubt challenge us to go now and do what we have learned in our journey through his book.

The story comes to mind of a patient in the Kennestone Regional Hospital who knocked over a cup of water, spilling it on the floor beside his bed. Afraid he might slip on the water when getting out of bed, the patient asked a nurse's aide to mop it up. Unbeknown to the patient, though, the hospital policy said that while small spills were to be mopped up by the nurse's aides, large spills were to be mopped up by the hospital's housekeeping group.

Well, the nurse's aide defined the spill as a large one. Consequently, she called the housekeeping department.

But when the housekeeper arrived, she declared, "I can't clean that up, it's a *small* spill. Our department only does *large* spills."

"In a pig's eye," the aide barked. "It's not my responsibility—it's a large puddle."

The housekeeper disagreed. "Well, it's not mine," she said, "the puddle is too small."

Back and forth they fired potshots.

The exasperated patient listened for a time, then took a pitcher of water from his night table and emptied it on the floor.

"There," he said, "is that a big enough puddle now for you two to decide?"

Have you ever noticed how often people try to shirk responsibility? It happens not only in the workplace but in the church as well.

"It's not my job!" grumbles one church member. "I don't have the time," says another. "Isn't that the pastor's job?"

As a pastor I've sometimes thought about how nice it would be to dump a pitcher of cold water on the quibbling saints. The fact is, though, that we all have a responsibility in God's family. I don't care if you're young or old, rich or poor, Republican or Democrat—God needs *you* to get to work. "Be a doer of the Word," James tells us, "we got enough hearers of the Word."

When every one of Christ's professed followers respond to His call for action, I believe we will see the fulfillment of Ellen White's vision for the church: " 'I have been deeply impressed by scenes that have recently passed before me in the night season. There seemed to be a great movement—a work of revival—going forward in many places. Our people were moving into line, responding to God's call. My brethren, the Lord is speaking to us. Shall we not heed His voice? Shall we not trim our lamps and act like men who look for their Lord to come? The time is one that calls for light-bearing, for action.' "[54]

I want to be a part of that "great movement," don't you? So what's it going to take?

It will require a remnant of people in the last days that respond to God's call for action. That means taking responsibility for whatever God calls you to do.

Maybe it means you'll serve on a church committee, or go as a missionary, or mop up messes as a volunteer at a local hospital, or donate your portfolio to the poor, or praise God in your trials, or wisely manage your mouth.

But whatever it is, for your sake, for God's sake, just do it!

[1] Charles R. Swindoll, "The Great Divorce" (sermon 134A), October 20, 1974, First Evangelical Free Church of Fullerton, California.

[2] John Ortberg, *The Life You've Always Wanted* (Grand Rapids, Mich.: Zondervan, 1997), p. 219.

[3] James Dobson, *New Man* (October 1994), p. 36, quoted from http://www.sermonillustrations.com/a-z/s/suffering.htm.

[4] Malcolm Muggeridge, *Homemade* (July 1990) quoted from http://www.sermonillustrations.com/a-z/s/suffering.htm.

[5] Tim Hansel, *You Gotta Keep Dancin'* (Elgin, Ill.: David C. Cook, 1985), p. 87.

[6] Philip Yancey, *Reaching for the Invisible God* (Grand Rapids, Mich.: Zondervan, 2000), p. 284.

[7] Quoted by Brad Mitchell in "Part 3, Give Us Daily Bread" (sermon C0019), Willow Creek Community Church, South Barrington, Illinois.

[8] John Ortberg, *If You Want to Walk on Water, You've Got to Get Out of the Boat* (Grand Rapids, Mich.: Zondervan, 2001), p. 179.

[9] Jerome Groopman, M.D., *The Measure of Our Days* (New York: Viking, 1997), pp. 63–87.

[10] Max Lucado, *When God Whispers Your Name* (Dallas: Word, 1994), p. 23.

[11] Dean Ornish, M.D., *Love and Survival* (New York: HarperCollins, 1998), p. 140.

[12] Max Lucado, *Just Like Jesus* (Nashville: Word, 1998), pp. 36, 37.

[13] John Ortberg, *Love Beyond Reason* (Grand Rapids, Mich.: Zondervan, 1998), p. 40.

[14] Quoted from http://www.sermonillustrations.com/a-z/a/anger.htm.

[15] *The Bottom Line,* as quoted from http://www.sermonillustrations.com/a-z/a/anger.htm.

[16] Quoted by John Ortberg in "Part 7, A Faith That Works, Doers or Hearers" (sermon M9808), Willow Creek Community Church, South Barrington, Illinois.

[17] Louise Hannah Kohr, *Insight*

[18] Jerome Groopman, M.D., *The Measure of Our Days* (New York: Viking, 1997), p. 169.

[19] Groopman, pp. 169, 170.

[20] Mother Teresa, *Words to Love By* (Notre Dame, Ind.: Ave Maria, 1983) as quoted from *Bible Illustrator* software (Parsons Technology).

[21] Author unknown.

[22] John Ortberg, *The Life You've Always Wanted* (Grand Rapids, Mich.: Zondervan, 1997), p. 211.

[23] William Barclay, *The Letters of James and Peter* (Philadelphia: The Westminster Press, 1976), pp. 7, 8.

[24] As told by John Ortberg in "Building Compassionate Hearts" (sermon M0023), Willow Creek Community Church, South Barrington, Illinois. The story is also published in *If You Want to Walk on Water, You've Got to Get Out of the Boat* (Grand Rapids, Mich.: Zondervan, 2001), pp. 89, 90.

[25] Charles Trumbull, *The Life That Wins,* 26, quoted by Dwight Nelson in *The Eleventh Commandment* (Nampa, Idaho: Pacific Press, 2000), p. 50.

[26] Bill Hybels, *Making Life Work* (Illinois: InterVarsity Press, 1998), pp. 16, 17.

[27] Adapted from Charles Arcodia, *Stories for Sharing* (Newtown, NSW, Australia: E. J. Dwyer, 1991), pp. 35, 36.

[28] Stephen Covey, *The Seven Habits of Highly Effective People* (New York: Simon and Schuster, 1989), p. 22.

[29] Lloyd John Ogilvie, *Let God Love You* (Dallas, Tex.: Word, 1974) as quoted in *Bible Illustrator* software (Parsons Technology).

[30] Ellen White, *Testimonies on Education,* p. 216.

[31] Maria Puente, *USA Today,* 19 July 2001, 2D.

[32] Quoted by Charles R. Swindoll in "How Fights Are Started and Stopped" (sermon 140A), December 1, 1974, First Evangelical Free Church of Fullerton, California.

[33] John Ortberg, quoting Bill Hybels from sermon manuscript, "It All Goes Back in the Box," October 15, 2000 (sermon M0042).

[34] As quoted in *Bible Illustrator* software (Parsons Technology).

[35] Stephen Covey, *The Seven Habits of Highly Effective People* (New York: Simon and Schuster, 1989), p. 89.

[36] Author unknown.

[37] John Ortberg, *The Life You've Always Wanted* (Grand Rapids, Mich.: Zondervan, 1997), pp. 119, 120.

[38] Quoted from *Bible Illustrator* (Parsons Technology).

[39] William Barclay, *The Letters of James and Peter* (Philadelphia: The Westminster Press, 1976), pp. 113, 114.

[40] Paul A. Cedar, *The Communicator's Commentary: James, 1, 2 Peter, Jude* (Waco, Tex.: Word, 1984), p. 90.

[41] Barclay, p. 116.

[42] Quoted by Lee Strobel in *What Jesus Would Say* (Grand Rapids, Mich.: Zondervan, 1994), p. 109.

[43] John Ortberg, "It All Goes Back in the Box."

[44] Robertson McQuilkin, "Living by Vows," *Christianity Today,* 8 October 1990, p. 38.

[45] McQuilkin, pp. 39, 40.

[46] McQuilkin, p. 40.

[47] Harold Kushner, *When Bad Things Happen to Good People* (New York: Avon Books, 1981), p. 117.

[48] Jack Riemer, *Likrat Shabbot,* as quoted by Harold Kushner in *When Bad Things Happen to Good People,* p. 118.

[49] Harold Kushner, *Who Needs God* (New York: Summit Books, 1989), p. 148.

[50] Richard Foster, *Celebration of Discipline* (New York: Harper and Row, 1978), p. 30.

[51] Richard Foster, p. 30.

[52] Marion Runge, "If I could have one wish . . ." *Adventist Review,* 28 January 1982. Used by permission.

[53] *Bits & Pieces* (January 1990), p. 15, quoted from http://www.sermonillustrations.com/a-z/s/speech.htm.

[54] Ellen G. White, *Life Sketches of Ellen G. White,* p. 426.

Small Group Study Guides

By Troy Fitzgerald

Chapter 1:

God's Blueprint for a Better Life

1. When was the last time you caught yourself preaching what you don't practice?

2. The author holds that it is not works that save the Christian but works mark the Christian. Why do you think the two ideas tend to get confused?

3. Who do you know that is someone you would like to imitate? What character qualities and principles do they live by that make them remarkable people?

4. "If your deeds don't show your faith then your faith is useless." How do you think most Christians would respond to that statement? How do you think the non-religious or secular person would respond to that statement?

5. What are some of your initial expectations and hopes for your own personal growth as you consider the topic of this book?

6. What issues in the introduction of this book do you think will be most rewarding for you? What themes will most likely present challenges to you and your current walk with God?

7. Reflect on the circumstances that have led you to pick up this book. Maybe it was a gift, maybe you know the author, and maybe it just seemed like something you need in this season of life. As you consider where you are at right now, what makes you confident about God's leading in your life? What are some things you are uncertain about? Pray a prayer as you begin and give God permission to speak to you and invite Him to engage you in the abundant life.

Chapter 2:

Your Pain, Your Gain

1. What trial or challenge have you endured that seems to be pivotal in your relationship with God?

2. As far as enduring through adversity is concerned, who has been an inspiration to you? Describe their attitudes and behaviors during their trials.

3. "Consider it pure joy when you face trials." What changes in attitude, perspective, or behavior need to happen in your life before you can do this and mean it?

4. Many have suggested that God "allows" trials to come your way. Others suggest that trials are intentional scenarios that God initiates. What are the difficulties with either view?

5. The author suggests that when trials come, instead of asking "Why?" ask God for wisdom. How do you think the approach that the book of James suggests would change the quality of your life? How does looking for the lesson instead of the reason for trials deepen your experience with God and people around you?

6. What is your definition of wisdom? Who in your life is an example of one who receives their wisdom from God?

7. To what degree does "the crown of life" in James 1:12 motivate believers to be faithful during difficult times? How does our future hope as believers motivate us through the difficult moments we are living through right now?

8. Where are you now? Reflect on the trials or challenges you face today and consider your options for enduring, growing, overcoming, and rejoicing in your trials.

Chapter 3:

Living Like Gilligan on Temptation Island

1. Share some of your observations about how modern culture has lost its innocence.

2. What kind of temptations do you handle head on? What temptations do you need to flee from? Why do you think the different responses are appropriate for the different temptations you face?

3. Think of a moment in your own experience this last year where you were victorious in resisting or fleeing?

4. What is your response to the research Stanford University conducted on four-year-olds and temptation? Did the results surprise you? Why or why not?

5. Being realistic about temptation is one of the strategies for overcoming. How does being aware of the spiritual warfare taking place around you equip you to resist? What temptations would you be able to resist if you were simply mindful of them while they were taking place? Which temptations are more a matter of will power for you?

6. Consider this statement: "The life you live becomes the legacy you leave, but only you can choose it." How does taking responsibility for the temptations that come to you fortify you to resist temptation? In what ways do people shirk the responsibility of the shortcomings in their spiritual life?

7. How does the "evil desire" become a slippery slope for people? When have you been able to recognize the initial workings of an evil desire in your heart? How did you respond?

8. Read James 1:15. Why is the illustration of conception and birth an appropriate tool for describing the way we are tempted? In verse 18, "The Word" is what gives the Christian a "reborn" experience. Consider how God's Word has enabled you to triumph over temptation recently. What moments would you like to re-live with God's Word prompting your decisions instead of your own weak-willed heart?

Chapter 4:

Relationships 101

1. Think of a time in the last few weeks when you were in a conversation but not really listening.

2. As you consider the ways in which Jesus listened (look, ask, touch), when in your life have you had people listen to you with more than their ears? How did that shape the way you felt at that moment?

3. Of the three ways to listen, which action comes more naturally to you, and which is the least natural way for you to respond? Why do you think this is the case?

4. In regard to relational wisdom, becoming slow to speak is invaluable. Have you had an experience like the one that took place in the doctor's office? If so, when?

5. Do you think being "slow to speak" is primarily for people who are constantly talking? Can you be silent in a conversation and still be inattentive? Sometimes our minds can disengage from honest listening and pursue another track without saying a word. What are some ways the church can foster an authentic openness in its relationships? In the way they communicate?

6. Temper Temperature: Which are you more like, a hot-tempered time bomb or a slow-stewing pressure cooker? In light of the counsel in this chapter, what practical things can you do to quell your anger when it is stirred?

7. In what ways have you seen anger short-circuiting relationships? What types of attitudes or behaviors can make you unhealthily angry?

8. As you reflect on the relationships that challenge your faith the most, set some specific goals that are based on the advice of this chapter to better manage the way you relate to others. Share some of those goals with a partner, friend, or anyone who will be willing to hold you accountable to the goals that you set.

Chapter 5:

Mirror, Mirror in the Word

1. What deed or act of kindness has left an indelible impression on you? Why?

2. What facts, truths, or beliefs of the Christian faith are easy to internalize and agree to, but are difficult to practice?

3. Why do you think people tend to become content with simply hearing the Word instead of doing it? What is it about our society that promotes this value system?

4. Consider how the Christian's beliefs and actions have an impact on the perceptions of non-believers about God.

5. The following principle is underlined in this chapter: Small things (like the tongue) can have a huge impact on the whole. How is it that the tongue can be so damaging to others?

6. Why do words have such tremendous power over people? Consider how difficult it is to build people up with words alone and how easily words can tear down and destroy. Why do you think this dynamic exists in relationships?

7. The parable of the man who held up the cross demonstrates how the deeds of our hands speak more forcefully than words. How is this true for you?

8. To what degree does doing works of kindness with our hands keep us from being polluted by the world? How does this principle work?

9. What comes first for you: the action of goodness produces a pure heart? Or the converted and purified heart promotes acts of kindness from your hands?

10. Make a list of three responses to this chapter. How will you use words this week to dispense grace to others instead of words that destroy? What will your hands do this week to bring a blessing to another person's life? What will you do to foster purity in your heart this week? Set specific goals.

Chapter 6:

Country Club Christianity

1. When have you ever been made to feel like "Gomer Pyle at a banquet of five-star generals"?

2. How does an elitist attitude destroy the potential for community? What major foundations does favoritism erode?

3. Explain what you think to be fundamentally wrong about favoritism? Of all the sins and shortcomings to point out, why does the Bible speak so plainly about favoritism? (See James 2:1.)

4. What are the prejudices that you see clearly in society today? What elements of prejudice are not so obvious but equally destructive to the life of the church? What is the theological or spiritual truth that motivates every believer to love and look at people unconditionally?

5. Why is it "wise" from merely a practical standpoint to not show favoritism?

6. From a biblical standpoint, describe why prejudice or favoritism is contrary to life in God's church.

7. What elements of favoritism do you want to eradicate from your heart today? What elements of elitism can you thwart in your community with specific activities? What are you going to do to make your church a place for *all* believers to be united and equal?

8. Reflect on the role models or godly people you know who demonstrate unconditional love. What can you do to imitate them? What difference do you think it would make in your relationship with Christ?

Chapter 7:

Extreme Faith

1. Consider the boldness of the statement, "Faith without works is dead." How can we believe that we are saved by grace through faith alone and reconcile that belief to this statement?

2. Which biblical story of faith best demonstrates how works authenticate faith?

3. How are the biblical stories of faith similar? How are the stories describing aspects of extreme faith different?

4. How does the chart enable you to make sense out of the different ideas that come from the writings of Paul as compared to James?

5. What do you think are the components of extreme faith? How would you define it in your own words or with your own story?

6. What illustration in this chapter was most inspiring to you? Why?

7. If it is true that "You can measure what you would do for the Lord by what you do," then how do you measure up today?

8. In what area of your life do you want to apply action to your faith?

9. Reflect on your own spiritual journey and meditate on the times when you felt God's presence was most real to you. Were those moments when your faith was active or passive?

Chapter 8:

How to Lick Your Tongue

1. When in your life have you ever said something thoughtless you wish you could have retrieved? Have you ever had an experience like the story of the seminarian at the beginning of this chapter? What happened?

2. If you were to analyze the content of your most serious conversations in the last month or two, what themes would emerge? What topics do you think would reappear? Was there a particular theme or soapbox sermon you have been musing over lately? Why do you think James is back with the topic of the tongue again?

3. The analogies of the horse's bit, the rudder of a ship, and the single spark that starts a fire describe what principle of life?

4. According to Christ in Matthew 12:36, 37, our words have the power to set the course for our destiny. Follow this truth in your mind and see if it bears out. Describe how the process of our words steering our lives works.

5. What are some words or phrases you would like to hear yourself say more often? What are some words or phrases you would like to eliminate from your conversations? Make a short list of each.

6. The power of the tongue to destroy is illustrated by the biblical terms James uses to indicate an unquenchable fire. What makes words so effective in destroying or building? How true is the saying, "Sticks and stones may break my bones but names will never hurt me"?

7. When in your life have words of positive affirmation made a significant difference in your spiritual growth?

8. If you were to use words to disclose what is in your heart, how would others describe the tenor of your life right now?

9. As you reflect on the things you would like catch yourself saying, consider also the affirming words others have said about you recently. Write a letter this week or make a phone call to someone solely for the purpose of honestly and graciously affirming him or her.

Chapter 9:

Time to Wise Up

1. When in your life have you ever mindlessly ignored or thrown away something valuable? Describe how you felt when you became aware of your folly.

2. When in your life have you ever stumbled onto an unsuspected treasure? How did you respond?

3. In the book of Proverbs, wisdom is described as being more valuable than silver or gold. Given the opportunity to live life over from the beginning with more of wisdom or wealth, what do you think most people would choose? Why?

4. What is your personal definition of wisdom? How does your definition compare to those mentioned in this chapter?

5. Who are the heroes of wisdom in your life? What particular attitudes, behaviors, or tendencies made you choose them?

6. What is the source of or basis of worldly wisdom? When have you seen this wisdom at work in those around you?

7. What is the source or basis of heavenly wisdom? Rank the seven qualities in the order of how you want them to appear in your life right now. Which ones do you need most?

8. Reflect on the qualities mentioned at the end of this chapter and think of specific areas of your life where those qualities need to be applied.

Chapter 10:

Got Conflict?

1. Share a story from your own experience that demonstrates how you tend to deal with conflict.

2. Which of the three causes of conflict would you say is most prominent in causing conflict in your life?

3. As you look at the conflicts that surface in your life, what are some of the more superficial reasons you might give for the problem? What are the deeper, more meaningful sources of the problem?

4. What do you think is the source behind why people look outside of themselves for what is responsible for their conflict?

5. In what relationship do you need to become more proactive (inside out)?

6. The first step suggested as a cure for conflict is submission. As you look at the examples given as to what that might look like, which one seems to strike a chord in your heart right now?

7. The second suggestion addresses the need for confession. When in your life have you experienced the freedom that comes from coming clean with who you really are? How was that experience helpful for you?

8. As you reflect and pray this week, consider James 4:10 to be a reminder to you of what makes us ready to resolve conflict.

Chapter 11:

Facing the Future

1. What experiences have you endured that remind you of how tentative life is and how fleeting time's passage can be?

2. How do you see people pretending to be in control of their life when life is clearly uncertain? How do you think God feels when He sees His children living so arrogantly?

3. Who has modeled for you the tender balance of preparing for the future but living each day releasing their grip of control to God's will? In what specific ways have you seen this evidence in their lives?

4. How is knowing God's will more about knowing God than anything else?

5. If God's ultimate plan for your life is to live in an abiding relationship with Him day by day, how does that affect your outlook on the future? How does this perspective shape the way you make the little choices and the big ones as well?

6. What biblical character comes to mind who seems to live with life's uncertainties yet manages to walk in step with God?

7. Reflect on all that you hope for in the future. What are the big goals and outcomes you hope to realize? Imagine what your days would be like if you placed as much emphasis on what is God's will for your life today as you do on the future. How would the quality of your life change? How would it remain the same?

Chapter 12:

Who *Really* Wants to Be a Millionaire?

1. Think of some examples of people in history (or in your immediate sphere of family and friends) who became corrupt because of their love of and focus on wealth?

2. Think of an individual you know who has great wealth but exemplifies a balanced view of the true value of things. Where do you think they learned the lessons of futility and the temporary nature of riches?

3. As you think of the people who are remembered throughout history as pivotal players for good, are those people remembered because of their riches or for other qualities? What qualities do people really remember after your life is over?

4. James comes right out and declares the temporary and empty value of a preoccupation with riches. How does a person whose mind is set on wealth ever experience conversion?

5. What is fundamentally destructive about the way many passionately pursue wealth?

6. What will it take for us to "gather the pieces of the game" and put them all back in the box?

7. Reflect on the reality of an eternal home in heaven with the Savior and how it puts all the "stuff" we strive after into perspective. What activities and exercises can you engage in to remind yourself of what makes our lives meaningful and successful on earth?

8. What can you do this week to demonstrate a renewed love for the life God has given you and a more realistic perspective of money?

Chapter 13:

Crockpot Christians and Bristlecone Believers

1. Who, in your circle of family and friends, is the picture of patience and peace in the midst of the storm? What life principles or character qualities do they exhibit that make them candidates for Crockpot Christians?

2. How much of our ability in the areas of patience and perseverance is part of our personality and to what degree do we develop the qualities as life skills?

3. Why do you think James chose the analogy of the farmer to illustrate patience? What other analogies would you use to make the concept clear to the readers?

4. James 5:8 uses the second coming of Christ as a reason to be patient. How does the soon return of Christ deepen our patience level? Do you think people are living anxious lives as they think about the time of the Second Coming?

5. What can you tell about the believers who are reading this letter, given the abrupt style of James?

6. How do you feel about the fact that Job is our "poster child" for preparing for the coming trials?

7. Who do you know that can be described as a Bristlecone Believer?

8. Think about a season of your life when you held on to God although the circumstances were dire? How have you become a different person because of your persevering? In what season do you wish you had been more determined in your hold on God through trials?

9. Reflect on the big picture of God's greatest desire for you. How do you see trials and the gift of patience making you a more effective Christian in the future?

Chapter 14:

Practically Praying

1. Which statement fits your understanding of the purpose and power of prayer the most: "Prayer moves God into action" or "prayer moves my heart into the right attitude?" If the two statements were extremes on a continuum, where would you place yourself? Why?

2. If God were to transform one area of your life through prayer, what do you think would be His focus? Why?

3. What story would you share from your life that demonstrates the reality that prayer works?

4. What story would you share if you were asked to demonstrate how prayer doesn't work? How have your prayers seemingly gone unanswered?

5. How would you like to see your prayer change for the better the things you will need to do? What do you expect God will do?

6. As you reflect on the exercises and inspirational moments of this book, how has your walk with Christ deepened and become more significant?

Chapter 15:

Living Proof

1. In what specific areas of church life is your congregation more like a sauna for saints?

2. In what specific areas of church life is your congregation like a high-impact exercise facility?

3. As you read the last chapter of this book, what new insights came to mind that you had not thought of before? What idea or challenge became the most thoughtful reminder? Why?

4. What ideas or stories proved to be an affirmation of how God was working in your life?

5. What ideas challenged you to re-orient your lifestyle the most? What plans do you have to continue to grow in those areas?

6. What three relationships in your life do you think will be strengthened most by this study? Why?

7. What character qualities do you hope to grow as a result of this study?

8. Reflect on the overall message of this book. What do you think might happen to your church family if everyone were to take to heart the advice of the brother of Christ and "just do it"?